HUME PAPERS ON PUBLIC POLICY:
Volume 5 No. 3

INNOVATION, INCENTIVE AND REWARD:
Intellectual Property Law and Policy

THE DAVID HUME INSTITUTE

HUME PAPERS ON PUBLIC POLICY:
Volume 5 No. 3 Autumn 1997

INNOVATION, INCENTIVE AND REWARD:
Intellectual Property Law and Policy

EDINBURGH UNIVERSITY PRESS

©David Hume Institute 1997

Transferred to digital print 2010

Edinburgh University Press
22 George Square, Edinburgh

Typeset in Times New Roman by WestKey Limited, Falmouth
Printed and bound in Great Britain by
CPI Antony Rowe, Chippenham and Eastbourne

A CIP record for this book is available from the
British Library

ISBN 0 7486 1074 X

Contents

Foreword	vii
Copyright: Over-Strength, Over-Regulated, Over-Rated? *Sir Hugh Laddie*	1
Industrial Property - Industry's Enemy? *Sir Robin Jacob*	17
Copyright as an Economic Incentive *Ruth Towse*	32
Biotechnology: Facing the Problems of Patent Law *Graeme Laurie*	46
Intellectual Property and the Internet *Charlotte Waelde*	64

Contributors

Sir Hugh Laddie is a member of the High Court of Justice in England and Wales and one of the Patent Judges.

Sir Robin Jacob is a member of the High Court of Justice in England and Wales and one of the Patent Judges.

Ruth Towse is a member of the Department of Economics at the University of Exeter.

Graeme Laurie is a member of the Department of Private Law at the University of Edinburgh.

Charlotte Waelde is Assistant Director of the Legal Practice Unit at the University of Edinburgh.

Foreword

During the last couple of years, the English Patent Judges, Sir Hugh Laddie and Sir Robin Jacob, have made a number of highly critical comments about current developments in the law of intellectual property. Many of these remarks were drawn together in their Stephen Stewart Memorial Lectures, delivered at the Intellectual Property Institute in London in 1995 and 1996 respectively. Although the lectures looked at very different aspects of intellectual property law, certain common threads emerged very clearly. One was that there was now too much intellectual property protection, and that this was bad for industry, trade and competition. The second thread followed logically from the first: the present law should be examined critically to see if it was performing its function properly, while any proposals for extension of intellectual property protection should be similarly considered with great care before translation into law. Thirdly, the assessment of both current and proposed law was not just a matter for lawyers. Just as important, if not more so, were the economists, who could engage in the research needed to measure the effect and effectiveness of intellectual property law. Equally significant were the intended beneficiaries of the protection, the creative and inventive persons in society together with those who transformed their ideas and information into products in the market-place.

This last theme in particular seemed to point the way for The David Hume Institute, which has always provided a forum for the fruitful inter-action of lawyers and economists and the practical application thereof, and has additionally had previous occasion to reflect on the subject of intellectual property. The Institute accordingly set about arranging a conference at which could be taken further the issues raised by the English Patent Judges, and the present issue of *Hume Papers on Public Policy* is intended to provide background material for that conference as well as being itself an independent contribution to the debate. The conference took place on 31 October 1997 under the same title as this collection.

A few words of background may be necessary for the reader without prior knowledge of the basics of intellectual property law. There are three major topics embraced under the general heading of intellectual property: copyright, patents and trade marks. In addition, this collection also refers to at least three other intellectual property topics, namely the protection of performers, industrial designs and plant varieties. The basic idea behind all forms of intellectual property is that the beneficiary gains an exclusive right to reproduce certain ideas, information and concepts which he or she has generated. While others can therefore be prevented from making such reproductions, the real value of the protection lies in the ability of the beneficiary either to market associated products directly, gaining a reward commensurate with the value the market places on those products, or, for an appropriate return, to permit others to manufacture and market the product. Intellectual property is thus traditionally seen as providing a means whereby the creative and inventive may be rewarded for their work, and so also giving an incentive for such work to take place.

Copyright is primarily concerned with the creative in literature, drama, music and art, although the minimum level of creativity needed is not high. In the twentieth century, protection has been extended beyond the traditional "author-work" to cover the media in which creative works are presented to their public: films, sound recordings, broadcasts and cablecasts. Problems have arisen increasingly as technological developments facilitate reproduction and dissemination, legal and illegal, of copyright material. Recently the length of copyright protection has been extended: in the case of "author-works", from the lifetime of the author plus 50 years to the lifetime of the author plus 70 years, while for "media-works" the period is 50 years from fixation or transmission, as the case may be. At the same time copyright law has had to grapple with the implications of yet another technology through which ideas and information can be conveyed to the public, namely computer technology, which, with its mighty array of software, databases and the Internet, poses a range of issues for discussion.

Patents exist for the protection of inventions. Where copyright is automatic, arising with the creation of the work, patents are granted only upon application to the state, embodied in its Patent Office. Before grant takes place, an application is subjected to rigorous examination testing whether the criteria of patentability are satisfied. A patent gives an exclusive right of commercial reproduction, and is thus again narrower in scope than copyright; but whereas infringement of copyright requires copying, a patent enables its holder to prevent even completely independent production. In the UK, as in most western European countries, the right lasts for 20 years from the date of application. Patents are excluded from certain areas, notably computer programs as such, immoral inventions, plant and animal varieties, and essentially biological processes for the production of plants and animals which are not micro-biological processes or the product of such a process. These exclusions have caused great difficulty, not only in relation to the burgeoning computer technology mentioned in relation to copyright, but also with regard to the remarkable recent developments of biotechnology and genetic engineering.

Although the fundamentals of trade marks remain broadly unaffected by the technological developments which have had such an impact in copyright and patents, the law here has also changed in response to the modern world, in particular the ever more sophisticated ways in which goods and services are marketed and reach their ultimate consumers. Trade marks are badges of identity which enable a customer in choosing between competing products to link them with their producers and the quality which is associated with those producers. Recent legislation has greatly extended the kinds of badges of identity which can be protected: things formerly excluded but now potentially protectable include the shape of containers such as the Coke bottle, sounds, tastes and smells. Like a patent, trade mark protection is obtained through a process of registration with the state, and certain criteria have to be satisfied before the grant is made, meaning that applications are carefully examined by the granting authority and will not necessarily be successful. Once obtained, however, the protection is potentially perpetual, although it has to be renewed every 10 years. It is available against the use by others of the same or similar marks in relation to the same, similar or even dis-similar goods and services. In Britain, unregistered marks may also be protected through the action of passing off, but here the claimant has to satisfy a court (through which alone protection can be sought) that the market associates the mark with him or her, whereas registration eliminates that requirement.

A further key dimension of intellectual property is that it may be capable of protection on a world-wide basis. Copyright arises in every country which is a member of the Berne Convention 1886. The owner of an invention or a trade mark can apply for patent or trade mark protection in many countries throughout the world by virtue of other international conventions. The protection thus obtainable is protection under the laws of the country where it is sought; but a major effort has been going on for some time to establish certain general minimum standards for national intellectual property laws, the most significant of which is the Agreement on Trade-Related Aspects of Intellectual Property Rights (TRIPS), signed as part of the GATT Agreement in 1994. The overall effect is growing convergence of national intellectual property laws around the world.

There have been even more far-reaching developments in the European Union. Community intellectual property rights are struggling into existence to supplement, and in the very long run perhaps to supplant, the national rights already existing in the Member States. The Community Patent Convention 1975 has never been brought into force, but a Community Trade Mark and a Community Plant Variety Right are now operative and may soon be followed by a Community Industrial Design Right. The failure of the Community Patent has been offset by the success of the European Patent Convention (which is not limited to the EU countries). This enables a bundle of national patents in Europe (as distinct from a single patent for the whole Community) to be obtained through a single application to the European Patent Office based in Munich. The Convention also establishes minimum standards of substantive patent law, and the European Commission now wishes to carry this further with a Directive on the protection of biotechnology. There are further potential Directives on the harmonisation of the laws on industrial designs and utility models (a lesser form of patent). Harmonisation through Directives has also been the chosen approach to copyright in the European Union: those already enacted have concerned computer programs, extending the term of copyright as noted above, rental rights, databases and certain aspects of satellite broadcasting. Further Directives on copyright issues are anticipated, dealing in particular with issues raised by the Internet, and the vexed questions of "moral rights", notably the artist's resale right or *droit de suite*.

In this collection, we have first reprinted the texts of the lectures by Mr Justice Laddie and Mr Justice Jacob referred to at the beginning of this introduction. These texts first appeared in the *European Intellectual Property Review* and the *Intellectual Property Quarterly* respectively, and we are grateful to the publishers of these journals, Sweet & Maxwell, for consenting to their re-publication here. Mr Justice Laddie provides a wide-ranging critique of the development of copyright. It is a monopoly which fetters competition and distorts trade, and the question arises as to whether this is justified by the benefits which it also brings to society at large, especially when the further extension of copyright is under consideration. This is considered in the context of the protection of industrial designs, the length of the copyright term, Crown copyright, scientific research, the criminality of certain infringements of copyright, and the limitations of fair use exceptions to copyright. It is argued that too much now receives the protection of copyright. The presumption should be against protection until it is objectively justified.

Mr Justice Jacob develops this theme across a wider range of intellectual property topics. If intellectual property is the law of private monopolies affecting industry in its widest sense, its expansion needs to be justified by proper research, in particular by the research of economists. He considers aspects of patent and trade mark law in this light, and is particularly critical of the recent European proposals for petty patents and artists' resale rights (*droit de suite*). He also raises a crucial question about the relationship between intellectual property and research and development work: does the protection of intellectual property encourage or inhibit such activity? To what extent is the availability of the protection important in the transformation of basic research into commercially successful products?

The judges' lectures are followed with three by Ruth Towse, Graeme Laurie and Charlotte Waelde. Ruth Towse fits Mr Justice Jacob's bill in that she is an economist currently researching the effect of copyright and performers' rights. She surveys the economic literature on copyright, and points out that much of it assumes a harmony of interests between author and publisher; but because copyright is a bundle of rights which have differing financial values, the parties' incentives and relative bargaining power in fact vary, leading to principal-agency problems. One response has been the creation of collecting societies by right-holders, but their operations, while reducing transaction costs, have increased concern about the copyright monopoly. The economic approach to such questions is by way of cost/benefit analysis, but the empirical data is lacking. Nonetheless a start can be made through the publicly available material on the activities of collecting societies. This suggests, however, that copyright does not provide a strong financial incentive for artists.

Lawyers provide the two remaining papers. Graeme Laurie discusses in some depth the difficulties with which the startling developments in biotechnology have confronted patent law. He illustrates Mr Justice Jacob's concern about the breadth of patent claims in an analysis of the recent decision by the House of Lords in *Biogen v Medeva* (a case notable, incidentally, for judicial reference to economic literature), while at the same time pointing out the problems in the development of a common European approach to such matters to which that decision may give rise. Mr Laurie shows how a relatively hostile stance towards the protection of biotechnology has left Europe unattractive to biotechnology investors, in contrast to the position in the United States, and argues for the adoption of a strong economic policy encouraging and protecting the industry. The moral issues surrounding biotechnology - research into "life", cloning, and so on - in essence concern the act of creation, not protection as such, and should therefore not find expression through the patent system.

Charlotte Waelde surveys some of the intellectual property issues arising from the development of the Internet, having particular regard to its impact upon commerce. The Internet provides a world-wide marketplace in which suppliers of goods and services are naturally very interested. Ms Waelde argues, however, that commercial interests are deploying the intellectual property rights which undoubtedly exist in "cyberspace" as elsewhere to transform the nature of the Internet as a general forum in which ideas and information are freely exchanged. This individual freedom, she argues, should not be sacrificed on the altar of commercial interests. Her survey touches on copyright and trade mark questions, and also shows the significance of an international response to problems which cannot by their very nature be answered by merely national laws.

The collection undoubtedly raises more questions and issues than can be answered and treated within its short compass; but that reflects both the current state of knowledge and the nature of the work as background to a conference intended to take the matter a little further forward. The David Hume Institute, while as ever eager to respect the intellectual property of its contributors by disclaiming all responsibility and denying any agreement with what this work contains, is delighted to be able to assist in the promotion of an important debate by the publication of these papers and the mounting of its conference.

Hector L MacQueen and Brian G M Main
Directors
The David Hume Institute

Acknowledgement

The David Hume Institute is grateful to Sweet & Maxwell for permission to reproduce the articles by Mr Justice Laddie and Mr Justice Jacob, which first appeared in [1996] 17 *European Intellectual Property Review* 253 and [1997] 1 *Intellectual Property Quarterly* 3. Further details of these journals are available from Sweet & Maxwell, 100 Avenue Road, London NW3 3PF.

Copyright: Over-Strength, Over-Regulated, Over-Rated?

Sir Hugh Laddie

Synopsis

Copyright is a monopoly which fetters competition and distorts trade, and the question arises as to whether this is justified by the benefits which it also brings to society at large, especially when the further extension of copyright is under consideration. This is considered in the context of the protection of industrial designs, the length of the copyright term, Crown copyright, scientific research, the criminality of certain infringements of copyright, and the limitations of fair use exceptions to copyright. It is argued that too much now receives the protection of copyright. The presumption should be against protection until it is objectively justified.

* * * * *

The purpose of this lecture, given in honour of the memory of a clever and perceptive copyright lawyer, is to consider the current state of copyright law in this country. Does it meet current commercial needs? My purpose this evening is to ask questions and possibly raise doubts. Copyright is one of the quartet of monopolies which form the core of what is now known as intellectual property law. The others, of course, are patents, trade marks and registered designs. I suppose that since the introduction of the unregistered design right in the 1988 legislation, there really is a quintet of such rights. Each, in its own way, places a fetter on the right of others to compete in the market-place with the originator of the right or his employer. Therefore, to some extent, each distorts trade.

If this were all, these monopolies would work against the interests of the public at large. At the simplest level it can be said that the existence of a monopoly enables the monopolist to increase his prices or restrict supply as he pleases. Of course, we know that that is much too superficial a view. It ignores all the benefits to the public at large which can flow from the increased creativity and investment which are the produce of a well-balanced monopoly system. But we must always bear in mind that monopoly legislation is the end result of a balancing act: is the restraint on competition justified by the benefits which it gives to society at large? In this lecture I would like to consider this basic balancing act as it applies to copyright.

A little history

One form or another of restraint on the printing and distribution of books has existed since the early sixteenth century. Until the eighteenth century it usually took the form of a monopoly granted by the Crown. It was used for almost 200 years as a form of censorship. The Government used it to suppress or control the distribution of books. Now most of us would say that was quite improper - Government should not control what we think or read. Statutory monopolies in a form recognised by us as copyright has existed in this country since the Statute of Anne in 1709. That legislation was introduced in response to lobbying by the book trade which said it was suffering at the hands of unlicensed copyists and that common law remedies were ineffective. In a style of lobbying which has become common since, it was said that the copyists were always men of straw and that it was impossible to track down even 1% of the copies. That Act created a copyright which lasted for 28 years.

The Statute of Anne sowed the seed of the legislation we now have. Over the years, paintings, engravings, sculptures and other aesthetic creations were brought within the reach of copyright protection. However, it appears that it is in the twentieth century that copyright has blossomed into a major monopoly with a commercial importance to match or even exceed that of patents. In this century we have had three major Copyright Acts and their sizes are a crude illustration of the growth of copyright and its reach. The Act of 1911 was a timid little creature. It contained a mere 37 sections. Some believe it was the best Copyright Act we have ever had. The 1956 Act was a more formidable affair. It contained 57 sections. It held sway during a period in which copyright litigation burgeoned. But the 1988 Act puts all of this to shame. It contains over 300 sections, about 280 of which relate to copyright and its new offspring, design right. This increase in size cannot be attributed merely to a trend towards verbosity in modern legislation, although there certainly is some of that present in the 1988 Act. To a large extent it reflects the spread and creation of new copyright-type rights.

Three sacred principles

There is nothing inherently wrong in having more legislation. Although we are now a much governed people, no doubt some legislation is worthwhile. The question which I want to consider is whether it is necessary or beneficial to have more of this legislation.

The existence of copyright is justified on three principles. The first is the Eighth Commandment: "Thou shalt not steal". Why should a trader who has expended nothing be entitled to reap where he has not sown? If Professor

Adams were to branch out into writing pop songs so as to augment his paltry academic income, or Mr Justice Jacob were to write maudlin poetry (of the sort we all know him to be capable of) to supplement his income as a judge, why should someone else be free to rake in the commercial benefit?

This ties in closely with the second principle. As Laurence Sterne expressed it in *Tristram Shandy*: "The sweat of a man's brows, and the exudations of a man's brains, are as much a man's property as the breeches upon his backside". The concept of owning matter created by the brain is perhaps the most fundamental foundation of copyright law.

But these two principles probably would not have resulted in the awesome width of current copyright legislation were it not for the third principle, namely the principle of reward. When it is suggested that any monopoly, whether it be patent, copyright or registered design, harms the public interest in free and open competition, the answer given usually includes the argument that the rewards furnished by the existence of a temporary monopoly are for the public good since they encourage the investment of time and money in research and development, and allow authors, musicians and the like to support themselves by their creative efforts. The result is that more artistic or inventive creations are made available to the public and the author or creator is encouraged to commercialise his output rather than keep it to himself as a secret.

The most obvious application of this principle is in patent law. Few currently challenge the argument that the existence of a lengthy monopoly period has been the foundation on which modern Western drug developments have been based. No company will put millions of pounds into medical research unless it believes that the product of that research will be protected and thereby offer the possibility of recovering the investment with interest. Comparison of Western drug developments with those in the Communist world have been held up as illustrating the value of the reward principle. However, even here there is a need for balance. It is not infrequently said that the rewards available from aggressively enforced patents have induced some drug companies to patent even non-inventive drugs as a means of keeping up prices.

This same principle of reward applies to copyright as well. Why would a record company spend millions in building, equipping and manning recording studios and pressing records or CDs unless it thought it could recoup the outlay from protected sales?

The growth of protection

I like to think of these as the three sacred principles. The question which I will put before you this evening is, "do these principles justify the current width of copyright legislation?" Let us start by considering how these principles have played a part in the development and expansion of copyright protection. Just as lobbying in the late seventeenth century and early eighteenth century resulted in the passing of the Statute of Anne, so it has been industry which has pressed and continues to press for greater and more effective protection against commercially damaging competition from copyists. In this century the

4 INNOVATION, INCENTIVE AND REWARD

growth of the entertainment industry has been significant. Entertainment is not now restricted to books and plays as it was in the nineteenth century. Now creative and artistic skills underpin a network of rich industries. Whether we consider records, computer software, satellite communications or television and films, the picture is the same. Just consider the example of a single large-budget feature film like *Jurassic Park*. It will have cost tens of millions of dollars to make. It will have been launched with the maximum publicity and merchandising support and it will be expected to generate an income of many millions of dollars. But such riches always attract the attention of those who wish to get rich without the effort of doing it themselves. Multi-million-pound industries selling dreams and pleasure to the public have inevitably attracted the attention of pirates. Similarly, few now will be ignorant of the intellectual, political and legal warfare which is being waged by the record industry against pirate CDs produced in the People's Republic of China - an anti-pirate campaign which has received strong and vocal support here. In the face of this type of unlicensed copying, there has been a persistent and well-received pressure to refine and expand the legal weaponry available both at the national and international level. In fact, there have been very few examples of significant restrictions being imposed on the scope of copyright. Nearly all changes to the law have been to make it wider and more powerful.

The major area of growth in the 1970s and 1980s was associated with the industrial application of copyright. Everyone now knows the basic story. It can be traced back to 1941 and the case of *King Features Syndicate v Kleeman* [1941] AC 417. That was the case in which it was definitely decided by the House of Lords that the copyright in a two-dimensional drawing could be infringed by copying it directly or indirectly and turning it into a three-dimensional article. In that case, the drawing was a cartoon of Popeye and the infringing three-dimensional article was an unlicensed brooch depicting the cartoon character. Any copyright lawyer worth his salt knew that original drawings were the subject of copyright even if they were functional and non-aesthetic. It followed that copyright subsisted in production drawings of mundane objects such as washers, screws and mechanical parts for cars. Indirect copies of such drawings were infringements of that copyright. The logical consequences of the King Features case and its potential commercial impact on the field of industrial design took a long time to sink in. However, a small Act, the Designs Copyright Act, passed in 1968 apparently to broaden copyright protection for jewellery manufacturers, acted as a catalyst. Very soon our courts and the courts in Commonwealth countries with similar copyright legislation were awash with cases where copyright in production drawings was used to afford proxy protection to industrial articles made to those drawings.

That this could never have been the intention of Parliament was not in doubt, but no court appeared to have the strength or perhaps the will to resist the tide. The first case on this development of the law to reach the House of Lords was *LB Plastics v Swish* [1979] RPC 611 in which the copyright in production drawings for knock-down furniture drawers was used to prevent one company copying the commercial furniture produced by a competitor. The response to criticisms that copyright could not have been intended to go this far was predictable. Copyright is only breached by someone who copies and no one is forced to copy. After all, weren't the defendants pirates? Furthermore, if the minor effort and skill which goes into a Popeye cartoon can be used to prevent the manufacture of cheap tinplate brooches, surely no lesser protection should be afforded to the greater effort, skill and precision which went into making production drawings for articles of commerce?

However, the onward progress of copyright appeared to be halted by the *British Leyland* decision ([1986] AC 577), in which the House of Lords discovered the existence of a previously unknown licence at common law which at least enables one trader to copy the spare parts for his competitor's machines. In that case, the House of Lords seemed genuinely shocked at the breadth and power of copyright protection. But, with the exception of the dissenting speech of Lord Griffiths, none of their Lordships felt able to attack the underlying principles as sanctioned in the *Popeye* and *LB Plastics* cases. The result was that industrially applied copyright continued to be used widely to prevent copying of commercial articles. The difficulty the courts experienced in moderating the law is illustrated by the *Lego* case ([1987] FSR 409; [1988] RPC 343, PC). You may recall that that was the case in which the well-known manufacturers of Lego bricks brought infringement proceedings against some Hong Kong competitors who were making copy bricks. The plaintiff had a number of difficulties in its path, including the fact that virtually all of its brick shapes had been the subject of registered design protection - which should have meant that the equivalent copyrights had expired. Notwithstanding this, both the High Court and the Court of Appeal upheld Lego's claim. It was only in the Privy Council that Lego lost, and then only by some imaginative legal argument.

Pushing back the tide

No doubt it was in part because of the BL decision and the growing chorus of complaints of those in British industry who were adversely affected by industrial copyright that the subject was dealt with by the 1988 Copyright, Designs and Patents Act. However, the way in which it was dealt with in that legislation is an illuminating illustration of how difficult it is to push back the borders of a monopoly once given.

One of the steps taken in the 1988 Act to overcome the perceived problems thrown up by the BL decision was to provide that spare parts were effectively removed from copyright protection. Secondly, copyright in the production drawings for non-aesthetic industrial articles could no longer be used to give proxy protection to the articles themselves. Surely then, at least in this area, copyright had been pushed back. But what about those in industry who complained that no one was forced to copy and that they had sunk time, effort and money into producing drawings and designs? Why shouldn't they be protected by the Eighth Commandment? Was the sweat of their brows and the exudations of their brains to be left to be pirated?

6 INNOVATION, INCENTIVE AND REWARD

The commercial reality was that from the early 1970s onwards many sectors of British industry had learned the pleasure of being able to prevent their products being copied. Under the protective wings of copyright they were able to fend off the attentions of cheap imitators. Trading without such competition is much more relaxing than having to meet the competition on price and quality. Furthermore, it was possible to argue that industrial copyright had protected British-designed products from cheap foreign copies - the xenophobic battle cry which always seems to impress legislators. This argument was never the whole truth. One of the problems with copyright was that it protected not only British production drawings but also, as a result of international conventions, American, Japanese and, in fact, most foreign production drawings too. And those who were stopped included British as well as foreign companies. The truth was that the United Kingdom and other Commonwealth countries became pockets where the normal cut and thrust of competitive copying did not run.

The arguments of those who had benefited from industrial copyright were not ignored. A new right was created called design right. But the new name should not mask the underlying creature. It is, in effect, a ten-year copyright available to protect any design or part of a design which is not "commonplace" - whatever that may mean. Furthermore, this new quasi-copyright is no longer founded on identifiable drawings. The plaintiff in a design right case can claim monopoly protection for the whole or any part of the design of an article of commerce. The new right is clearly intended to protect designs which have no aesthetic merit or input but are valuable for reasons of functional utility. One of the examples of a suitable candidate for protection given during the parliamentary debates was the design of the upturned end of an aircraft wing now to be found on some larger aircraft. The competitor will not know whether it is the whole or which part is suggested as being protected by the new rights until he receives a writ. I suggest that the creation of design right is an indication of the difficulties the legislature has of removing a monopoly in this field, once given.

The BL case highlighted one of the other major peculiarities of copyright law. Under the 1956 Act a copyright owner who sued successfully for infringement was not only entitled to damages, an injunction and delivery up of infringing articles, but also to conversion damages - that is to say, damages which approached the total value of the infringing goods sold by the defendant. Maybe damages on this scale made sense when only a very small percentage of infringements could be traced and where the interests of impecunious authors and composers were at stake, but virtually every legal commentator accepted that conversion damages were now an anachronism which had little justification where commercially exploited copyright was concerned.

Conversion damages were, of course, criticised by the House of Lords in the BL case. Such damages were available not only in industrial copyright cases but in all other cases as well, and their size was an enormous deterrent to infringers. I can say from my own experience at the Bar that in many cases defendants would rather settle than fight a doubtful claim for fear of losing and being saddled with a crippling liability to conversion damages. By the same token, the threat of conversion damages was a great benefit to copyright owners. They had a remedy which more than compensated them for any loss they may have suffered by reason of the infringement. Conversion damages were a non-compensatory penalty grafted on top of the copyright owner's right to obtain normal compensatory damages.

Well, with the passing of the 1988 Act, conversion damages disappeared. But did they go completely? I think not. To explain why, I must digress a little into another area of copyright law. In 1952 the Committee considering changes to the law of copyright recommended the introduction of a new head of financial relief in cases where, for example, the infringement had been flagrant. This recommendation was accepted and gave birth to section 17(3) of the 1956 Act. The Committee clearly thought that it was creating a new form of exemplary damages. One may ask the question why exemplary damages should be available against a flagrant infringement of copyright but not a flagrant infringement of patent or act of trespass or breach of contract. Indeed, a person who conspires to steal a consignment of computers will not be amenable to exemplary damages - but flagrantly to copy one of the operation manuals is quite another matter. The copyist of the manual is a pirate, after all, whereas the thief is only a thief.

I suggest that this too, is an example of the over-sensitivity of the legislature to the interests of copyright owners, a sensitivity no doubt based in part on the belief that copyright is for the benefit of authors, musicians and other worthy people who, as a class, might not be expected to be able to look after themselves. It was to protect them from the predations of those who were and are referred to collectively and pejoratively as "pirates". Anyway, section 17(3) provided that such flagrancy damages could only be awarded when the court is "satisfied that effective relief would not otherwise be available to the plaintiff". If effective relief was otherwise available, then no flagrancy damages could be awarded. The idea was to ensure that the copyright owner at least got something for the wrong done to him.

If one looks at the 1988 Act one finds that statutory exemplary damages continue to be available, but the drafting of the section has changed. In particular, the requirement that the plaintiff must show that effective relief would not otherwise be available has been removed. It is now easier to qualify for these damages and it is clear that they are designed to give the copyright owner financial relief over and above what is necessary merely to compensate for damage done. Why has this change been introduced? Examination of the parliamentary debates shows that it was intended as a form of quid pro quo to copyright owners who were unhappy at the abolition of conversion damages.

Term

These are just two respects in which modern copyright law provides, so some might say, an over-abundance of protection to the monopoly right owner. But there are others. Let me illustrate the point. If a company were to spend millions of pounds on finding and developing a new anti-cancer drug, it could apply for a patent. Securing patent protection would be a costly and time-consuming exercise. It would be necessary to show that the drug was new and inventive. The protection given would be for a maximum of 20 years. A design may be the subject of an application for registered design protection. Once again, some time and effort would need to be expended on the registration procedure and it would be necessary to prove novelty. If registration is achieved, the design will benefit from protection for a maximum of 25 years (increased in 1988, I might mention, from 15 years - an increase of 66%).

What about copyright? We all know that objective novelty is not required. We all know that registration is not required. Like the best things in life - it is free. But what about term? In the Act as passed in 1988, the term of monopoly is specified as life of the author plus 50 full years for literary, dramatic and musical works and a flat 50 years for computer-generated works, films, records and broadcasts. However, as a result of the Term Directive, the copyright in the first category of works, that is to say, literary works and so on, is now life of the author plus 70 full years. This additional 20 years has been imposed throughout the Member States of the European Union to bring us into line with the domestic law of Germany. As is now familiar in copyright law, the process was one of levelling up the protection rather than levelling down. The result of this new term is that if, for example, a young computer programmer writes a new piece of computer software, he generates a monopoly which will normally last for over 100 years. Depending on his longevity, it may last more than 150 years. Similarly, if a politician writes letters or speeches which are of general historic interest, they also may be protected for a century or more. Indeed, if a modern-day architect were to design a new Albert Memorial, he would have the satisfaction of knowing that his copyright is likely to be sprightly and in the prime of life long after the concrete and steel of his architectural creation have started to crumble.

The question to be asked is: what justification is there for a period of monopoly of such proportions? It surely cannot be based on the principle of encouraging artistic creativity by increasing the size of the carrot. No one is going to be more inclined to write computer programs or speeches, compose music or design buildings because 50, 60 or 70 years after his death a distant relative whom he has never met might still be getting royalties. It is noticeable that this expansion of term is not something which has only occurred in the last decade. On the contrary, it has been a trend which has been in evidence for the whole of this century. Before the 1911 Act, the term of copyright in artistic works extended to seven years after the author's death. In 1911 this was extended to 50 years after death. The growth of term is in fact greater than these figures suggest. Life expectancy in 1910 was far shorter than it is now. The result is that a monopoly which was expected to last about four decades in 1910 should now be expected to last on average more than three times as long.

Indeed, I believe that the same criticism of excessive duration can be levelled at the 50-year flat term which applies to films, recordings and broadcasts. It may be possible to pick out a few creations of exceptional artistic or commercial merit where one could argue for lengthy protection - for example, the recordings of Rostropovich or the Beatles - but is it right that all copyright should be protected on the basis of what might be thought justified for the exceptional few? Furthermore, it is possible to argue that these long copyright terms are not necessary to protect the commercial exploitation of the works themselves. Most works protected by copyright are exploited very rapidly, if at all. This is so whether we are considering films and records or literary works such as computer software. Even books such as those that win the Booker prize are only commercially successful for a short time and then, to all intents and purposes, pass away. Yet the dead hand of copyright lingers on, in most cases serving no useful purpose.

Another of the problems with copyright law is that, unlike inventions protected by patent or designs protected by registration, the requirements for qualification are so low as to be virtually non-existent. Virtually any written material, any sketch and any film footage or sound recording is automatically protected. This has practical consequences. In *Elanco v Mandops* [1979] FSR 46 the Court of Appeal accepted, as it had to, that a label of instructions placed on the side of a barrel of herbicide was a copyright literary work. No doubt depending on the youth of the literary genius who wrote it, the label will be protected for more than a century and perhaps for as long as a century and a half - certainly well beyond the date when for safety or commercial reasons the product has been removed from the market. So one of the troubles with copyright, then, is that it springs up to protect nearly every creation of the human mind, be it ever so trivial. As another member of the judiciary put it, the fact that our system of communication, teaching and entertainment does not grind to a standstill is in large part due to the fact that in most cases infringement of copyright has, historically, been ignored.

Let me offer you an illustration of the lack of balance in our law. You can libel a dead author to your heart's content, but if you want to honour him by publishing a commemorative edition of his letters, 50, 60 or 69 years after his death, you will infringe copyright, you may have to pay exemplary damages and, as I shall discuss in a moment, you may be prosecuted.

The bandwagon

Is it surprising that with ever greater monopolies being created and the awareness of them spreading, more and more want to get into the copyright exploitation market? Perhaps the strangest, but most symptomatic of these is the Government itself. First, many of you will know that the effect of section 301 of the 1988 Act is to grant a perpetual right to royalties in favour of the Great Ormond Street Hospital for Children in respect of the exploitation of J M Barrie's play, Peter Pan. It was no doubt thought a good thing that a source of income other than taxation should be found to support that worthy institution, but I suggest that the device of effectively granting permanent copyright in this case illustrates the imbalance when it comes to legislating in this area. Who can lobby against the widening of protection? Those who do are treated as pariahs and parasites. Why should they be allowed to exploit J M Barrie's creation without paying for it - even if stopping them means extending the copyright not for decades but for centuries?

Perhaps of greater significance is the Government's realisation of the value of the copyright it has bestowed on itself in a vast array of government publications, including Acts of Parliament. This has resulted in the Government seeking a royalty, for example, from those who wish to reproduce legislation - in legal textbooks or in electronic databases. But it does not end there. In *The Times* of 7 November 1995 there was a report, which I believe is accurate, that the Inland Revenue granted an exclusive licence under Crown copyright to one publisher to reproduce its tax manuals. Unfortunately, HMSO appears to have granted a non-exclusive licence to the same material to another publisher. The conflict of licences has been resolved, at least for the moment, by the HMSO terminating the licence to the second publisher and seeking an injunction to restrain it from making further use of the material. Of course, it would not be proper for me to say whether the HMSO is right as a matter of law in its attempts to terminate use of this material. But I do think it is legitimate to point out that the frenzy to get on the copyright bandwagon now extends to the legislature seeking to make money out of the exploitation of the legislation which it passes and which should be available for all of us to see and consult. The Government can now control the dissemination of its laws - does this represent a seed of the problem of censorship which we thought had been abolished 200 years ago?

I should make it clear that it is not just the Government which has been attracted by the ever-widening scope of copyright. Copyright has reached into many other areas. Perhaps the most depressing is the area of pure research. Until quite recently it was seen to be normal and desirable that scientists should share knowledge with their colleagues at symposia at the earliest possible date. New experimental results were disclosed to the community of scientific peers in this way. The plaudits of colleagues were reward enough. This system began to crumble with the realisation of the value of patents. Many senior researchers now no longer publish the results of their work in the scientific press or at meetings with their colleagues at the first opportunity. Now they, and the universities or hospitals they work for, make sure they have applied for patents first.

Copyright has now been harnessed to this desire to acquire proprietary rights in the result of research. As many of you may know, many able scientists are involved in research into gene structure. Some are trying to work out the genetic code of human beings - the fundamental blueprint which determines all of our characteristics. It is, I think, sad that some of them, including some of great eminence, are talking in terms of "copyrighting" that code or parts of it once it has been worked out. The object is to ensure that exploitation of that knowledge can be turned into a money-making exercise. But it is hard to argue that scientists should stand aloof when so many others are using the armoury of intellectual property rights, including copyright, to make money.

COPYRIGHT: OVER-STRENGTH, OVER-REGULATED, OVER-RATED? 11

Infringement a crime

So far I have discussed the width of copyright and two forms of financial relief available in infringement proceedings. But it is wrong to consider only the relief which is available in civil courts. Those of you who have hired video films may have noticed that, when the tape is played, a message comes up on the television screen which says "VIDEO PIRACY IS A CRIME". Well it is. Criminal provisions have been found in Copyright Acts for some years but now, apparently for the first time, they are being used in earnest. A recently reported case is illuminating. Criminal proceedings were brought against a book publisher and its directors. I think there were nine directors in all. One of them was the infirm 87-year old widow of the original founder of the publisher. The publisher had produced a book which contained reproductions of one or more copyright paintings. Difficult questions of fair dealing were raised as a defence. It might be thought that to bring such proceedings with complicated issues of copyright law before a magistrates' court did not make sense. However, I find it difficult to fault the logic of those acting for the private prosecutor. The Copyright Act stipulates that criminal procedures may be invoked against an alleged infringer and, in the case of an infringing company, its directors. Why not use these weapons?

If the proceedings had been brought in civil courts, it is almost certain that the directors would have been struck out of the proceedings since there was no evidence, at least in relation to most of them, that they had any personal involvement in the production of the offensive book. But the criminal provisions relating to directors in the Act are, to say the least, relaxed. And if it is permissible to bring criminal proceedings, why not do so? The threat of a criminal conviction hanging over an alleged infringer's head and the heads of its directors is much more likely to make them sue for peace than the mere risk of losing in civil proceedings. Like the prospect of being hanged, it does concentrate the mind. The fact that these statutory provisions are being used to enforce purely private commercial rights appears to be irrelevant. Furthermore, there is a great incentive to proceed in this way. The costs of the prosecuting copyright owner are usually paid out of central funds, even if the prosecution fails. This little bit of budgetary largesse has escaped critical scrutiny so far.

We have therefore reached the state where taxpayers' money is being used to enforce private rights which many might think are more than adequately protected by civil remedies. I should also mention that it appears that in most cases it is not the poor and weak who are using these criminal provisions but the rich and well organised.

Fair use

The reluctance to curtail the copyright monopoly also finds expression in the statutory defences provided by the 1988 Act. In the United States of America, there is, I understand, a statutory defence of fair use. Its limits are not precisely drawn, but it has given the courts the flexibility to prevent copyright from being abused. The absence of precision is, of course, a disadvantage. To some extent, the scope of the defence will be dependent on the personal perspective of the judge. However, I would suggest that a comparison between that system and our own is not flattering to ours. Let us consider this a bit further. The United States Copyright Act of 1976 contains, at section 107, a general statutory defence of fair use. It says that fair use of a copyright work for purposes such as criticism, comment, news reporting, teaching, scholarship or research is not infringement. It goes on to indicate some of the factors which the court should take into account in deciding whether use is fair. The factors mentioned are:

(1) the purpose and character of the use, including whether such use is of a commercial nature or is for non-profit educational purposes;
(2) the nature of the copyright work;
(3) the amount and substantiality of the portion used in relation to the copyright work as a whole;
(4) the effect of the use upon the potential market for or value of the copyrighted work.

As the US Supreme Court has said on more than one occasion, this fair use defence "permits courts to avoid rigid application of the copyright statute when, on occasion, it would stifle the very creativity which that law is designed to foster".

Compare that with our legislation. Rigidity is the rule. It is as if every tiny exception to the grasp of the copyright monopoly has had to be fought hard for, prized out of the unwilling hand of the legislature and, once conceded, defined precisely and confined within high and immutable walls. This approach also assumes that Parliament can foresee, and therefore legislate for, all possible circumstances in which allowing copyright to be enforced would be unjustified. Based on this approach, we now have an Act in which there are 49 sections of numbingly detailed exceptions to copyright infringement. Let me remind you of one or two examples.

Section 30 provides that fair dealing with a work for the purpose of criticism or review does not infringe copyright, but only provided it is accompanied by a sufficient acknowledgement. Sufficient acknowledgement means that the work has to be identified by title and author. In the absence of the whole acknowledgement, infringement follows even if the review does not harm and all the readers would be aware of both the identity of the work and its author. The requirement for sufficient acknowledgement applies if the criticism or review is in a newspaper, but not if it is in a film, broadcast or cable programme. But if it was not thought necessary for them, why make it a requirement for any other form of criticism or review? Section 32 provides that copyright in a literary, dramatic, musical or artistic work is not infringed by its being copied in the course of instruction or of preparation for instruction and is not by means of a reprographic process. In preparing this lecture, I had to be careful not to photocopy any material. Section 61 contains incredibly detailed provisions permitting the recording of folksongs, but only if it is for certain archival purposes. Apparently, it is permissible to archive folksongs but not any other songs. I am also afraid that archival collection of Mr Justice Jacob's poetry will still be an infringement. Section 63 provides that it is not an infringement of copyright in an artistic work to copy it or to issue copies to the public for the purpose of advertising the sale of the work. No doubt that is of assistance to Sothebys, Christies and other auction houses, but notice that the defence is not available if the work is merely to be hired. I invite the members of this audience to read for themselves the convoluted and essentially self-defeating provisions of section 50B which are concerned with decompilation of copyright computer programs.

These detailed and pedantic exceptions to copyright protection, and their predecessors in the 1956 Act, are not only difficult to understand in some cases, but they also reinforce the perception that virtually all reproductions of copyright works, no matter how innocuous, are infringements. Is it surprising then, that when, for the purposes of advertising the film *Carry on Cleo*, a poster was created which was a harmless but humorous spoof of a similar poster for the Elizabeth Taylor/Richard Burton film *Cleopatra*, it was held to infringe copyright.

It would be possible to go on criticising the width of our copyright laws, but perhaps I have said enough. It might be more useful to inquire why our law has developed as it has. I have mentioned already the value and size of the industries which now believe they need extensive copyright protection to safeguard their income stream. They, quite properly, lobby for their interests. But who lobbies against them? There is no trade union of copyright infringers. Support for any limitation on copyright is easily portrayed as support for pirates - the usual pejorative global expression for infringers. It is depicted as support for the parasites of industry. Is it surprising, then, that the scope of protection gets ever wider? I suggest that the drafting of the legislation bears all the hallmarks of a complacent certainty that wider copyright protection is morally and economically justified. But is it?

A balanced future

The whole of human development is derivative. We stand on the shoulders of the scientists, artists and craftsmen who preceded us. We borrow and develop what they have done; not necessarily as parasites, but simply as the next generation. It is at the heart of what we know as progress. When we are asked to remember the Eighth Commandment, "thou shalt not steal", bear in mind that borrowing and developing have always been acceptable.

I invite you to stand back and imagine that we were not building our copyright law on a foundation of accumulated rights, commercial interests and monetary expectations. Imagine that we have just a blank sheet of paper and are being invited to create a copyright law now from scratch for the new millennium and that the purpose is to give some reasonable measure of protection to those who write books or computer programs or make films for television. Would we really choose to construct a monopoly which might last a century and a half? Would we really make it a crime to copy even quite small parts of the copyright work throughout those many decades? Would we really choose to pick out copyright as the one monopoly where statutory exemplary damages are available? I think not.

But, if we are going to start with a fresh piece of paper, let us do a proper job and really start from first principles. I am sure that all of you here are familiar with the wide variety of materials which are now protected by copyright law. I have already mentioned *Elanco v Mandops*, in which the list of instructions on the side of a tin of herbicide was protected as a literary work. But we also know that it has been suggested, in *British Northrop v Texteam Blackburn* [1973] FSR 241 that a well-drawn straight line or circle would be likely to be protected as artistic works. Indeed, we all know that during the great industrial copyright days of the 1970s and 1980s it was generally accepted that a drawing of, say, a washer - merely two concentric circles on a page - would be protected as an artistic work. In *British Leyland*, some of the drawings sued on, and accepted by a hostile House of Lords as being copyright works, consisted of simple depictions of a short straight length of tube. The law reports of the last 90 years are full of trite and insubstantial works being protected by copyright. How did we get to this position?

Was it always so? I doubt it. Most of us know that although most works have to be "original", it is now well-accepted law that "original" means that the work has originated with and is the product of at least a small amount of effort of the author. This can be traced back to *Walter v Lane* [1900] AC 539, in which the House of Lords held that copyright could exist in the notes of a speech of Lord Rosebery taken down by a shorthand writer in the audience. The original effort involved in transcribing was said to be enough to justify copyright protection. I think it is likely that the current view of originality was not always the law. In *Dicks v Yates* (1881) 18 ChD 76, the Court of Appeal had to consider whether the words "Splendid Misery", the title of a book, were covered by copyright. It is quite clear that the then Master of the Rolls, Lord Jessel, thought that a literary work could only be "original" if it was original in a patent novelty sense when compared with what was already available to the public. The fact that the same words had been used by another author some 80 years previously therefore destroyed originality. Similarly, Lush LJ said:

> I take it to be established law that to be the subject of copyright the matter must be a composition of the author, something which has grown up in his mind, the product of something which if it were applied to the patent rights would be called invention.

Whether *Walter v Lane* ever justified the wide scope given to originality now is beside the point. It is the law. But if we were to start again, to mould it closer to the heart's desire, would we really choose to give the full armoury of copyright protection to the trite, the commonplace and the valueless? Whatever the law was in the last century, the costs of reproduction probably went a long way to ensuring that litigation was normally restricted to copyright works of substance - *Dicks v Yates* being one of a handful of exceptions. But we now live in a world where everything is recorded in computers or made available on the Internet. Everything is recorded and the public has begun to learn of the existence of the free and spontaneous monopoly it gets under copyright.

The usual response to this sort of criticism of the breadth of copyright protection is to say that if a work is trite, its copyright is of less value because third parties can get to the same end result by working it out for themselves. But this is just another version of the pernicious refrain: "You are not forced to copy and what is worth copying is worth protecting". I suggest that this approach is facile and unconvincing. The fact that a trite subject-matter can be arrived at independently is no reason for giving it a monopoly. We should not be handing out monopolies like confetti while muttering "this won't hurt". I suggest we should approach monopolies from the other direction. We should say, as our predecessors did, that the basic rule is that no monopoly should exist unless it is shown to be objectively justified.

Maybe the time has come to look forward, rather than backwards. Perhaps we should consider whether the current law on originality makes sense or serves a useful purpose. To reduce it to its simplest, you can have too much of a good thing and I suggest we have got too much copyright. In the case of copyright, the Eighth Commandment has got out of control. If you go to a restaurant and taste the creation of one of our new breed of flamboyant chefs, say beef with a sauce of mango and pickled parsnips, would you consider it immoral to go home and try to make the same thing? If a friend tells you a good joke, is it immoral to write it down in a letter to a relative? If you read in a newspaper the details of evidence given in a high-profile trial, do you consider it theft to take the essential elements and write a poem about it? Do you know of Mr Robert Fosbery? He was a man who, after much trial, a lot of effort and, no doubt, considerable pain, worked out that it was possible to jump over a higher high jump if he jumped over backwards - the Fosbery Flop. He broke all sorts of records with his new technique. And then along came copyists and did it better. Were they immoral? These examples are meant to be light-hearted - but I give them to illustrate the point that not all copying is bad and that, sometimes, copying and developing are to the general good. I should make it clear that I believe copyright has an important role to play in society. I do not advocate an unprincipled free-for-all. But I suggest that the scales are at the moment weighted far too much in favour of would-be copyright owners.

At the beginning of this lecture I referred to the Popeye case. It is reported in the 1941 volume of Appeal Cases. At the beginning of that volume there is another case dealing with another area of law. It contains the well-known statement of Lord Atkin: "When these ghosts of the past stand in the path of justice clanking their mediaeval chains, the proper course is for the judge to pass through them undeterred" ([1941] AC 1 at 29). In relation to a statutory monopoly like copyright, it is not open to a judge to pass through undeterred. He must apply the law. But it is possible to see that in the case of copyright not only do the mediaeval chains remain, but they have been reinforced with late twentieth-century steel. Perhaps the time has come when we should look again at the underlying assumptions on which this monopoly is based.

16 INNOVATION, INCENTIVE AND REWARD

* * * * *

This is the text of the first Stephen Stewart memorial lecture, given on 29 November 1995. It first appeared in [1996] 17 European Intellectual Property Review 253-260 (Sweet & Maxwell), and permission to reproduce it here is gratefully acknowledged by The David Hume Institute. Since the lecture was delivered, there has been a significant change of policy with regard to Crown Copyright and its exercise, details of which are available from The Stationery Office.

Industrial Property - Industry's Enemy?

Sir Robin Jacob

Synopsis

Intellectual property is the law of private monopolies affecting industry in its widest sense. The expansion of these monopolies needs to be justified by proper legal and economic research. This theme is illustrated by assessment of patent and trade mark law, as well as by consideration of proposals for droit de suite.

* * * * *

This is the second Stephen Stewart memorial lecture. I am honoured to be asked to give it. I wish he was here to discuss with us the problems upon which I touch this evening. He would have had a lot to say.

When I was asked for a title I gave my answer instantly over the telephone. The sponsors, Butterworths, in due course e-mailed back. Did I mean "industrial property", or had the word "intellectual" got garbled over the telephone? I e-mailed back the word "industrial". I will tell you why at the outset.

The general area of law now called "intellectual property" is in the main a law conferring private rights on one party to prevent competition from others. It is fundamentally about industry - an economic law - a law that controls or forms the base for industrial activities. To call it "intellectual" is misleading. It takes one's eye off the ball. "Intellectual" confers a respectability on a monopoly which may well not be deserved. A squirrel is a rat with good PR. Is "intellectual property" perhaps a phrase coined by the same PR agent for monopolies? One senior member of Chambers used to say when I was starting, "We are the grit in the wheels of industry". That was perhaps too cynical a view, but it is right to say that so-called intellectual property is the law of private monopolies affecting industry in its widest sense. It should be viewed in that light.

Last year Sir Hugh Laddie's lecture (above) was confined to copyright. He called it "Copyright - Over-Strength, Over-Regulated and Over-Rated". The title was meant to contain a question mark, but it was clear from his lecture that he regarded copyright as having gone too far. He pointed to its entry into the control of industrial design, to the vast period of copyright protection of 50 years from the death of the author being increased to the even vaster period of 70 years from death, to the extraordinary remedies of additional damages, to the danger then threatened of the government regarding the very laws of the land as being property to be charged for, and to the low level of originality required by our law. Fortunately the government has now retreated somewhat and as a result it is to be hoped that modern methods of containing and displaying statutes - CD ROMs, and on-line services - will not be imperilled by threats of Government applications for injunctions. But that is a matter of concession only. Even so it remains the case that transcripts of reserved Court of Appeal judgments bear the doubtful, but menacing, claim, "Crown Copyright" on their title page.

Sir Hugh indicated his own considerable unease at the present scope of copyright. The question I put before you today is whether that unease should apply to other areas of intellectual property, and if so what should be done? Are intellectual property laws, originally intended to strengthen creativity, innovation, investment and enterprise, getting out of hand? I not only share Sir Hugh's unease about copyright - I think there is justification for unease over the whole range of the subject. I indicated my unease in my Foreword to the Intellectual Property Institute's Newsletter in January 1996. I said:

> However justified the cry "what we need is protection" may be for an anti-AIDS campaign, it is not self-evident for a process of the creation of new or escalated kinds of monopoly.

Sir Hugh and I are not alone. The next Newsletter of the Institute found Lord Hoffmann also raising questions about where intellectual property is and where it is going.

What I propose to do this evening is to examine some current topics in the field of industrial property, generally focusing on particular examples. There will be a constant theme - Intellectual Property Rights need properly researched legal and economic information before they are imposed. I also propose to mention one or two hobby horses of my own.

Patents

I begin where Sir Hugh left off. He ended his lecture by giving the Fosbery flop as an example of a case where not all copying is bad and that sometimes copying and developing is good. He thought that was self-evident. But inside a year two young and bright American lawyers, Scott Kieff and Rob Kundstat (1996),[1] have suggested, in an article entitled "It's Your Turn, but My Move", that novel athletes' moves (leading for instance to being able to pitch a baseball 10% faster) are patentable. They argue that there is no difference in principle between this and any other innovation - particularly, in the case of sports, innovations in equipment. They also suggest that copyright may have a part to play in sports - regarding movements as something like choreographed movements of dance. Looking at some Olympic so-called sports, one can see their point. Similarly, even if it seems difficult to imagine a new way of heading a soccer ball, it is not difficult to imagine a new way of celebrating a goal. Indeed sometimes it seems that that is the primary occupation of some players.

Kieff and Kunstat finally suggest that there might be some trademark or like protection available to novel athletic moves. The important point to note about their article is that it is not absurd - legally speaking. This sort of "protection" is coming within the range of the guns of intellectual property. And I suggest that it is doing so because people have stopped asking what intellectual property is for and whether it is doing any good.

Another example from the field of patents. As many of you will know, the Federal Court of Appeal in the USA has held in *re Alappat* 33F 3d 1526 (1994) that computer programs as such are, essentially, patentable. And there is complaint from the US that the European Patent Convention (EPC) forbids the patenting of such programs as such. This is despite the protection given by copyright and the fudges which allow hardware when programmed to be patentable in some circumstances. Now what is instructive if one reads the Federal Court judgments - both the majority and the powerful dissent of Chief Judge Archer - is the lack of any measurements to support or refuse protection. One finds economic assertions made but not justified. Likewise, when the British Patent Office held a Symposium in 1994 on legal protection for software related innovation, whilst there was a majority in favour of patents for computer programs, the *reasons* for the majority view remained essentially assertion of benefits rather than proof. Some may intuitively feel that the computer program industry has in no way needed a patent incentive to encourage innovation. It has and continues to blossom at an astonishing rate. And the problem of properly defining claims and searching prior art might (as Archer CJ suggests) prove to be a mighty hindrance to the industry. Likewise the combination of protection with the adoption of standards (e.g. the increasing dominance of Windows) may suggest that the anti-monopolists - the anti-trust brigade - should step in. The truth seems to be that no-one actually knows. What is certain is that the protaganists of "protection" have a loud voice. But then they would, wouldn't they - for they are principally the lawyers of the big battalions.

My next example in the field of patents is one which I mentioned some time ago in my Herschel Smith lecture. This is the problem of "undue" width. As you will know, the Patents Act 1949 and its predecessors (ultimately the common law) explicitly contained the notion that you cannot patent more than you have invented. In the language of the 1949 Act, a claim had to be "fairly based" on the matter disclosed in the specification. Under Article 84 of the EPC a claim has to be "supported by" such matter - but - and this is surprising to many - once a patent has been granted there is no objection to validity as such upon this ground. One has an intuitive feeling that something ought to be done about it. And now something has. It has taken twenty years for the ingenuity of the European Patent Office (EPO) and, last week, our House of Lords, to get round the problem by a hardly self-evident stretching of the Convention. The arguments are roundabout and over-elaborate ways of dealing with the perceived problem of undue width. Both the EPO and the Courts (look for instance at what can only be described as soul-searching by the Court of Appeal in *Genentech* [1989] RPC 147) are worried by over-large claims. They have been, until last week, finding ways of cutting them back based on an intuition of an economic harm caused by over-large claims. Last week that which was intuitive and unexpressed was, for the first time, made explicit. Lord Hoffmann in *Biogen v Medeva* [1997] RPC1 expressly looked at an economic analysis of over-large claims in holding that the Patents Act permits claims to be struck down on this ground. The analysis was American. I am not aware of any European analysis of the problem, which I think is considerably under-researched. Further, I believe that so far as our intellectual property jurisprudence is concerned, this is the first time a court has looked at an economic analysis in deciding what the law should be. I very much doubt whether one study is enough. Is undue width really a problem, and if so in respect of what sorts of claim? Surely it is not beyond the wit of modern research techniques to find out. Or must judges (and Patent Offices) go on working largely by intuition? The investigation should be how actual supposedly over-large claims actually affect industry's behaviour. There will be an economic angle to this too - do the owners of over-large claims make too much money from them?

My next patent example relates to the much discussed "use" or "for" claims. The Enlarged Board of Appeal of the European Patent Office, in *MOBIL/Friction reducing additive* [1990] OJ EPO 93; (1991) 22 IIC 85; [1990] EPOR 73 approved a claim in the form "Use of compound X as a friction reducing additive in a lubricant". This was so even though it was known to add X to a lubricant for the purpose of rust inhibition. No-one knew that X also reduced friction until the patentees found that out. It is not my intention to go into the merits of this decision now. Why should I when the House of Lords skirted the point in *Merrell Dow*? My point in referring to the case tonight is to look at the real justification for the decision. This was an inarticulate major premise in the decision itself. It was made articulate by one member of the Board later. Mr Paterson (1996), in a lecture to the 1994 European Patent Judges' Symposium, said: "Use claims provide protection for research into the further properties of known products, especially chemical and pharmaceutical products". Now what I want to know is whether what is implied by that assertion is true. The Editors of the European Patent Office Reports said when they reported the case: "Claims of this type, now that they have been formally sanctioned by the Enlarged Board of Appeal, may be expected to proliferate". Well have they?[2] Is it really the case that research on "inherent" results of old processes is impeded by lack of prospects of a patent? Has the decision in *MOBIL* made the slightest difference to the direction of research? The decision is now six years old and one ought to be able to find out. In the words of *Private Eye*, I think we should be told. Similar questions arise in relation to the effect of the second medical use type of claim. This has been established much longer. So firm results should be discoverable.

At this point, I propose to take a diversion from my main theme tonight to put forward a proposal. The need for it is exemplified by *MOBIL*. It is self-evident that there are intellectual and practical difficulties with *MOBIL*-type claims from the infringement point of view. Mr Paterson suggests that infringement would involve what he calls "an element of subjectivity" - but that is not readily to be found in the provisions of the Community Patent Convention (CPC) from which national laws of infringement are derived. It is easy enough for the EPO to side-step the difficulties. It is not an infringement court. And the Enlarged Appeal Board is not staffed by judges. One of the things I would like to see is a change in the composition of the Board. I think its legal members should be national judges with patent experience. The Board sits on comparatively few cases a year, and so the judges could go "on circuit" for the short periods necessary. They would have the expertise and experience to consider how claims would be treated in national courts. The decisions of a Board so composed would be likely to command respect throughout Europe and to have a significant effect on the harmonisation of the European patent system. As Mr Paterson (1996:190) observed in his discussion of *MOBIL*.

> Since the legal framework within which the EPO works is not exactly equivalent to the framework within which each national court works, the achievement of a harmonised European patent system in the absence of a truly integrated system cannot be easy.

I believe my proposal, if implemented, would result in a significant degree of harmonisation of the patent system. Judges who work together are much more likely to think together or at least along closely similar lines. So not only would the opinions of the Enlarged Board have an enhanced status but in other areas of law, both substantive and procedural, an increased mutual understanding and a common approach would be likely to emerge. I think from my own experience that the meetings of European Patent Judges which have been organised by the EPO have shown the way. I am glad to say that I think I have benefited very much from such meetings. I know Sir Hugh agrees, and I hope and believe our European colleagues from other countries feel the same way.

My last patent example relates to employee inventions. Sections 39-42 of the Patents Act 1977 provide for employee inventions in various ways. In particular there is provision for what is called "compensation" for an employee who has made an invention which is of outstanding benefit to his employer. If the invention was patented, then the employee is to get a "fair share" of the benefit. The thinking behind the provisions was in part that employees would have a greater incentive to invent and in part some sort of general equitable fairness. There are similar provisions in Germany. I have a number of questions. Does the UK system work? How many employees are getting compensation? How much is being paid? I suspect the answers are "few" and "little". Certainly there are few reported cases on the provisions, and I can hardly believe that this is because most the claims are resolved without any formal dispute. Assuming the provisions have failed, does this matter? Is the incentive theory valid? Is more paid in Germany, as I believe it is? What is the effect in research departments in Germany, and particularly are there fights to be named as inventor? What about US and Japanese company employee inventors? Is the whole theory of the thing a mistake? It is only hard research, not speculation, which can begin to answer these questions. Yet they are important. If a system of extra reward for successful inventions was a real and effective spur to employee inventors then surely, if our existing provisions do not work, they should be made to. And if such a system is not effective or is not shown to be so, then let us get rid of it as having been no more than an emotive but ultimately pointless scheme.

Droit de suite

I wish next to consider proposals for *droit de suite* and second-tier protection. These are proposals from the Commission of the European Union. Let me de-politicise what I have to say at the outset. The days are long gone when each nation state can simply create its own intellectual property laws regardless of what the corresponding laws in other countries may be. The requirements of international trade demand a drive towards harmonisation. Even if there were no European Union, it would be necessary to harmonise. The European patent system - a non-Union system - is an example of just that. So, though I criticise the two individual proposals, my criticisms do not go any further than that. I believe that we Europeans are right in trying to work together in trying to forge rational intellectual property laws which actually have the effect of furthering innovation, creativity, and investment in Europe. My attacks on the specific proposals have two bases. First, there is my individual perception that their implementation will run counter to these very objectives. More importantly, I wish to point out with all the force at my command that neither proposal has anywhere near justification in objective economic-based practical research.

I begin with *droit de suite* or the artist's resale right. The idea is simple enough: painters and sculptors often, when they are young, sell their works at a comparatively low price. Later they may become famous and so the works increase in value. But they get no share of that increased value. The idea is that the original artist (or his heirs - for the right is to last as long as ordinary copyright, namely the vast period of 70 years from the year of death of the author) should have a percentage of every subsequent sale of his work. The right is to be inalienable. The justifications for the rule are set out in the draft Directive. In part the recitals consist of mere assertion, and in part very doubtful assertions of economic effects:

> Whereas, in the field of copyright, the artist's resale right is an inalienable right enjoyed by the author of an original work of art or original manuscript to an interest in any sale of the work subsequent to the first transfer by the author.

This assertion of an inalienable right is the conclusion, not a justification for the conclusion. Thus in the case of a literary work, the author is free to sell his copyright at the outset. Why not the manuscript too? This proposed right is the first inalienable right since the bizarre rule that the last 25 years of a copyright was inalienable until the author died. This widows and orphans provision of our 1911 Act did not, so far as I am aware, actually achieve much. Maybe some widows and orphans got something, but no-one knows. And if they did, it is by no means clear why they deserved it.

I go to another recital:

> Whereas the artist's resale right is intended to ensure that authors share in the economic success of their works; whereas it helps to redress the balance between the economic situation of authors and that of other creators who benefit from successive exploitations of their works.

But if a painter becomes famous, his later paintings become worth more. You can't buy a new Hockney now for what one cost in 1964. Successful painters do benefit from successive exploitations of their works. First, it is that which puts up the price of their current work. Second, they retain the copyright in those works and have rights in reproductions of their work. On the other hand, a painter's remuneration does not depend on how many people look at his picture. If you follow this idea through, then there should be a painter's fee for looking at his picture in a gallery. And equally logically if the price of a work falls over time, the owner ought to be able to claim compensation from the painter.

The next series of recitals is about the need for harmonisation within the Community. This is very important and I want to discuss it further now before returning to *droit de suite*. The problem is this. It is much easier to harmonise intellectual property rights up than down. No-one minds being given more rights than they had before, whereas people are apt to complain very seriously - raising cries of destruction of property without compensation - if their rights are cut down. I am sure that the real reason for the increase in term of copyright to 70 years from year of death of the author was simply that it was easier to harmonise up. Publishers and copyright owners welcomed the unexpected and undeserved gift. No rights were taken away in Germany where they already had 70 years, so there were no problems there about destruction of existing property. Only the general public lost: not just financially but in other ways too. For instance, the reimposition of copyright for another 20 years had serious implications for scholarship. See for instance the powerful criticism of the Term Directive by a professor of English, Professor Patrick Parrinder (1993). He points out how the dead hand of copyright prevents the work of scholars in a variety of ways. Publishers cushioned by entrenched rights are not interested in annotated editions or correcting mistakes in existing texts: they just go on collecting the money.

So I think the Commission and Council should have courage. First, they should establish on the basis of facts a real need for harmonisation. If such a need really exists, then harmonisation down is the right way unless it can be shown that there is a real economic need for this right. The presumption should be *against* imposing or extending monopolies or like rights. Only harmonise up if a serious economic case for it is proved. Some might say that a good example of this was the introduction of Supplementary Protection Certificates increasing the term of protection for inventions such as pharmaceuticals which, for regulatory reasons, could not be marketed for most of the term of the normal patent life. SPCs encouraged investment in underdeveloped inventions and one can intuitively feel that they are probably justified on that ground.

Let me consider harmonisation further. Assume a policy of complete harmonisation for intellectual property laws throughout the union. Each country at present has its own laws. A thorough policy of harmonisation carried out only upwardly would require all countries to have a monopoly or like law if any one of them did. Thus our design law, both registered and unregistered, has no exact counterpart in other countries. Must our law be imposed on them to achieve harmonisation? And other countries have their laws of unfair competition of varying strength. Must the strongest of these be imposed on the whole Union? In some countries the legal procedural system makes it easier to obtain interlocutory injunctions than in others. Should we all grant such injunctions because one country does? And even that might not be enough. Why should parties be allowed to patent in only some countries of the Union? Surely if they patent in one, for the sake of harmonisation they ought to be compelled to patent in all - even if they can't afford it.

I return to *droit de suite*. I said that if it is to be imposed rationally, then a case must be made out for it first. Here we need a careful and precise economic analysis. That must be based on actual research. How much does *droit de suite* help young artists now in the countries which have such a law? How much would the law affect dealers and auction houses? Would business in expensive works simply leave the European Union (EU), particularly for Switzerland and New York? Why should non-EU vendors sell in the Union? What will be the costs of administration of this levy?

The Commission claims to have done some research. I am no economist, but what I have seen, the letter of 25 April 1996 from the Commission to the President of the Council, contains what I can only describe as a non-analysis of the position. There is no information as to what difference it would make to young artists, or indeed does make to young artists in countries which have the rule. No information exists as to the extent to which sales are made in non-*droit de suite* countries to avoid it, no information is given on the costs of compliance and administration. There is, however, a statement that some countries are unwilling to give up *droit de suite*. But since we do not know whether, in those countries, it has any practical effect, it is absurd to say that it should be imposed on those countries where it probably would - unless an economic case can be made out for it. There is an assertion of distortion of the market - but no proof or examination of why the art markets in non-*droit de suite* countries (hence on a level playing field) differ so much as between themselves.

What have artists themselves to say about *droit de suite*? Some are in favour. But have they really thought the thing through? The right sounds nice - more money for artists. But can that really be shown? How much would go to agents anyway? - you can't make cash inalienable.

Now I know there is a sort of emotional appeal which says that dealers exploit artists. Of course they do - but the artists could not be without them. Nor could writers do without publishers. Mere emotional response is not a good basis for legislation. And it can often have unintended consequences, as we all know. One of the unintended consequences here may well be a benefit to insurers, packagers and carriers as they take works out of the EU to be sold on the world market.

The conclusion is simple: the case for *droit de suite* is not made out. There has been nowhere near enough research or economic analysis. There ought to have been. One should not go about making a Community-wide monopoly or like rights without proper in-depth economic and quantitative studies. The Commission should go back to the drawing board. It should be looking at abolishing *droit de suite* - at harmonising down or simply leaving things as they are. It is a nice emotional idea, but in practice it may be worse than useless.

Petty patents

I turn to another proposal which I think suffers from exactly the same defects of inadequate research. This time that research is not merely inadequate in economic terms but also in legal terms. I refer to the proposal for "second-tier protection" or "utility models" or "petty patents". I prefer the last of these terms; the word "patent" conveys more properly what is being discussed, a monopoly right of some sort.

The general thought behind the idea is something like this: some ideas or mechanical designs are not inventive enough to be patentable. And anyway the costs and time of getting a patent are both substantial. So the patent system is not available for these "petty" inventions. The problem is particularly significant for small and medium size enterprises (SMEs): all too often they find their ideas copied and as a result they cannot find the capital necessary for investment. So what is needed is some lesser right than a full patent, a right which costs less, for instance because there is no examination.

It seems to follow as night follows day from the above that there should be a cheap system of petty patents. Indeed one can hardly imagine how so many countries have got on without such a system. Yet I have to say that it is my belief that the imposition of a petty patent system would cost us Europeans dearly. I say that from my many years' experience in practice and my more limited experience on the Bench. I am well aware that many lawyers may say otherwise. I suggest, however, that lawyers can only contribute to part of the debate - and probably the lesser side of it. When I set out the reasoning for the system, almost every statement leading to the conclusion was an economic, not legal assertion of fact.

First, consider the position of SMEs. Why should they be the winners if petty patents become possible Europe-wide? Big industry will take these out more readily than small industry - especially if they are cheap. A competent corporate patent department will not only apply for patents to cover the company's products, it will surround the patents with an outer defence wall of petty patents. A small man wishing to innovate will be able to get his petty patent cheaply - but will not know unless it is searched whether it is any good. And if he wants to market his new product, he is likely not only to have to search for patents but for petty patents too. And if the latter are unexamined, then he will have to take advice as to their scope and validity. The advice will include the cost of searching. And who will get the best advice - the big company or the little company? You will notice that I have here specifically included the costs of lawyers and patent agents in the costs of the system. They are all, of course, loveable and especially deserving people. But in economic terms they are a compliance cost of the intellectual property system. Industry has to pay for them. So far as I can see, compliance costs have not been taken into account at all.

Next, consider the position of the courts. The suggested petty patent is to be invalid if it is very obvious. But a patent is invalid if it is obvious and in practice a patent has to be pretty obvious before it is revoked these days. Under the old German national patent system a patent had to have sufficient "inventive height" - which may have involved more than mere obviousness. Anecdotally they had a higher standard than we did in the UK; in other words obviousness was easier to establish in Germany than here, both in the respective Patent Offices and the courts. That may have been enough to leave some room for a petty patent in Germany. But anecdotally at least, the EPO has not required the same inventive height as was formerly the case in Germany. And I for my part cannot see any room for clear water between current standards of obviousness for patents and some lesser standard for a petty patent.

In reality a petty patent will be just an unexamined patent, but with a lesser term, a less well-defined scope and very uncertain validity. It is likely to be a millstone round the necks of European industry, especially small and medium-sized industry.

What then does one say about the fact that a number of EU countries have a petty patent system? Well, I do not think we have anywhere near enough information about how they work in practice. It is no good just looking at the substantive law. That is the easy thing to do - you look at the formal provisions of the law. Apart from commissioning a report from an economic research institute in Germany, that is all that the Commission have done. What one wants to know is how the various systems actually affect research, innovation and investment. How do they actually affect big companies and little companies? Before one embarks on a EU-wide imposition of second-tier protection, these questions must be answered and answered satisfactorily and not by assertion. If one does not do that, one is embarking again on a harmonisation-up exercise without any or any sufficient justification.

This is no trivial matter. If this system is imposed on Europe and it turns out to be mistaken, it will be very, very difficult to go back. Petty patents, once granted, will not be removable. It really is worth organising a detailed study of what is best to do. The existing studies suffer from a number of defects. I will return to this point shortly.

In this country we have no experience of a petty patent system as such. But we did have something slightly comparable and indeed have it still. Mechanical inventions are often embodied in copyright drawings and, such was the overarching nature of copyright protection during the 1970s and early 1980s, that in practice copyright in industrial designs operated as a partial petty patent system preventing close copying of industrial artefacts. Again I have a question. What good or harm did the system do? Surely we can have more concrete answers than that "it prevented unfair copying". Did the system encourage innovation or investment? Or did it unduly cushion

INDUSTRIAL PROPERTY - INDUSTRY'S ENEMY? 27

companies into lazy reliance on the protection given so that their need to beat others in the market by novel design was reduced? Are there no ways of finding out by research? Incidentally, the repeal of the existing system and its replacement with a lesser system with a limited provisional provision is one of the few examples of a reduction in intellectual property rights in recent times. I commend it as showing that harmonisation up is not the only way. You can reduce intellectual property rights.

I said I would return to the existing studies. The Commission based its work on a study done in Germany by the well-respected IFO Institute. That study, the Commission's green paper, has been examined here for this Institute, by Dr Margaret Llewellyn. I have to say that Dr Llewellyn's excellent work really shows beyond doubt that the case for imposition of a second-tier system of some kind is far from made out. In part this is because the Commission has taken the IFO results further than they will legitimately go and in part because the original study is, I am afraid, rather too limited. If a system of such potential for impeding European industry is to be imposed, I believe that a much fuller and deeper study is called for. That such a study would be expensive is as nothing compared with the cost if the system is mistakenly imposed.

There is another reason for waiting. As you will know there are advanced proposals for an EU registered design system. I do not have the time to go into this. In principle again it seems a good idea. What worries me that it is to be added to other systems of "protection". It will undoubtedly cover some of the ground of a second-tier system, however theoretically different the sorts of right are supposed to be. And in our country it will add to unregistered design right. In others it might be added to unfair competition or like rights. Let us see how this goes before rushing into second-tier too.

Trade marks

Next I turn to trade marks. The Trade Marks Directive and the corresponding national legislation (ours is the 1994 Act) have sought to harmonise in part European Trade Mark Law. But at the same time there are many who seem to think that it has also taken trade mark law well beyond anything conventionally recognised as such. Let me give you two examples.

First, "Association". Can there be infringement if a defendant's trade mark merely brings to mind the plaintiff's, even though no-one thinks the defendant's goods or services have any trade connection with the plaintiff? Those who have read *Wagamama* [1995] FSR 713 and the articles and counterarticles in the *European Intellectual Property Review* by Mr Peter Prescott QC and Dr Kamperman Sanders will be familiar with the problem and will, I hope, forgive me for briefly summarising it. It arose in the following way. Wagamama is a well-known Japanese noodle bar. The defendants intended to open an Indian restaurant called "Rajamama". The plaintiffs proved that a significant number of people would think that Rajamama was not only an Indian version of Wagamama but also that it formed part of the same enterprise. So there was passing off. Laddie J also held that there was trade mark infringement because Wagamama was a registered mark. He could have stopped there. But, given that the subject matter of the dispute was restaurants, he decided to make a meal of things. He went on to consider what the position would be if people thought no more than that Rajamama was a sort of Indian Wagamama but did not think it was commercially connected with it. He said there would be no infringement in those circumstances. He held that the phrase in the Trade Marks Directive:

> "a likelihood of confusion on the part of the public which includes the likelihood of association between the sign and the trade mark"

meant only that a kind of association which led to confusion was an infringement.

Emotive language characterised the subsequent debate. Dr Kamperman Sanders (1996 a) started it by calling his first article "Back to the Dark Ages". He asserted that a trade mark is more than a trade mark. He asserted a "modern understanding that the trade mark itself embodies value as a conveyor of goodwill and quality, publicity or life-style". He coupled this with an assertion that any association with the plaintiff's mark ought therefore to be stopped as endangering this value. I believe that the real trade marks are a good deal more robust than that. There was some "association", for some, with Mr Stringfellow's nightclub when McCain's called their chips "stringfellows" but there was no damage of any kind. Kit-Kat and Kit-e-Kat have lived side by side for years. The tons of annual Kit Kat sales say that no-one worries about the association with cat food. Mr Peter Prescott QC (1996) hit back at Dr Kamperman Sanders with an equally emotively entitled article "Think before you Waga Finger". And Dr Kamperman Sanders (1996 b) replied with a more moderately entitled article "The Return to Wagamama" which was in its content fairly heated.

It is not necessary to go into the details further today. What I wish to say is that you can approach this question practically or in an abstract manner. My contribution to the debate is to ask, what can be proved as a practical matter for both sides? In particular, I suggest that the extended view of trade mark protection favoured by some theorists requires justification as a practical matter. The extension of monopoly rights by assertion of damage without proof will not do. Purely theoretical or abstract arguments have no place in forming the rules of intellectual property.

Can research help here? Is there anything which can be measured or shown justifying the extended view? If not, then it should not prevail. One could investigate, for instance, what trade marks in the "dark ages" were damaged by the kind of association favoured by the wide school of thought. If none, or only a few can be found, that would militate against the extended view of "association". After all, the traditional view of what trade marks do has, I believe, served industry well for a long time. Going further may well represent an unwarranted interference with the rights of others, another burden on industry. That burden relates not only to what cannot be done, but to the enormous costs of finding suitable marks. Compliance costs are an important matter all too often overlooked in considering what the law should be. What is the compliance cost of the extended view?

My next example relates to "distinctiveness". It is clear that under the new law containers may be registered as trade marks. This was barred under our old law of registered trade marks, but the law of passing off could clearly protect a distinctive container, as the Jif lemon case revealed. So far I have no problem. My problem starts when one sees what the UK Registry appears to be doing and what I fear the European Trade Mark Registry may do. People are coming along with funny-shaped bottles. They say: that's an unusual shape, a distinctive shape. So put my new bottle on the register. This, if followed through, will turn the trade marks registries into designs registries - nay, better than designs registries, for the monopoly given is permanent. I believe (and this is a mere non-judicial opinion without argument) that mere unusualness in a container shape does not make it *a priori* capable of distinguishing for trade mark purposes. Distinctive does not mean unusual; it means doing the job of being a trade mark. Whether or not a funny shape does that job can only be established by use and recognition as a trade mark. But suppose I am wrong. Does it matter if funny-shaped bottles can be registered on the nod for permanent monopolies? I think we need research here too.

Conclusion

I have covered a lot - probably too much - ground tonight. But I want to conclude by considering where this seemingly unstoppable drive for more monopoly has come from and how I see things developing.

So far as the drive is concerned I have to say that I think that too much of it has come from lawyers. Professor Goodhart summed it up in the title of his Chorley lecture this year: "Economics and the Law: Too Much One Way Traffic". Why has the traffic been one way in the case of intellectual property rights? These rights are complex not only in law but even more so in their practical operation. They are not readily understood even by businessmen, still less the general public. Businessmen have a terrible tendency to let policy be decided by lawyers. The attitude is: we have got an intellectual property department. Why keep a dog and bark yourself? The answer is that it is generally a mistake to let your dog run your affairs.

Also, I think there is a psychological trick at work here: it is somehow much more interesting to think about how you are going to stop others than to think about others stopping you. It is more fun to be a plaintiff than a defendant. And use of words like "protection" rather than "monopoly" encourages such thinking.

Further there is: lawyers studies of the problems can be over-academic. Often they are studied more because they are intellectually interesting than because they are important. Thus, the differences, if any, between the German and British approach to patent infringement remain the subject of almost perpetual debate. Yet this can only be of significance in marginal cases. It is a minor problem compared with a new second-tier system or what the rules for a European design system should be. And I have to say that I think even economists and other observers often look at problems or do studies at too general a level to be helpful in deciding what intellectual property laws should actually be. You can try to consider what intellectual property rights are worth in a general sort of way. But detailed research aimed at specific topics - e.g. the significance of use claims - is rare indeed.

As to the future, I think things are looking up. Economists are looking more carefully at legal rules and lawyers are looking beyond the law. It is my hope that we will see very rapid progress in this area and that future legislation and, perhaps, judicial decisions will be founded upon a more sold basis than has been the case in recent years. If that can be achieved, intellectual property will be the friend of industry, not its enemy.

* * * * *

This is the text of the second Stephen Stewart Lecture, delivered on 7 November 1996. It was first published in (1997) 1 Intellectual Property Quarterly 3-15 (Sweet & Maxwell) and The David Hume Institute is grateful for permission to reproduce it here.

Notes

1 At the time of writing they were Associates with a well-known UK firm of intellectual property lawyers and are now Law Clerks to that great judge and jurist Judge Giles Rich of the Federal Court of Appeal for the 10th Circuit. I am grateful to the authors for sending me a copy of their article and I hope they will forgive my using it as an example of intellectual property law going too far.
2 Only cases where a simple process claim is not available would count. Just tacking on a use claim when you have a valid process claim would not be relevant evidence of anything other than a sensible precaution by patent agents.

Bibliography

Goodhart, C.A.E., (1996). Economics and the law : too much one-way traffic? *Modern Law Review*, **60**, 1-22.
Kieff, S., and Kunstat, R., (1996). It's your turn, but my move. *International Law Journal*, 20 May.
Parrinder, P., (1993). The dead hand of European copyright. *European Intellectual Property Review*, **15**, 391-393.
Paterson, G., (1996). The novelty of use claim. *International Review of Industrial Property and Copyright*, **27**, 179-190.
Prescott, P., (1996). Think before you Waga-finger. *European Intellectual Property Review*, **17**, 317-321.

Kamperman Sanders, A.W., (1996a). Back to the dark ages. *European Intellectual Property Review*, **17**, 3-5.
- (1996b). The return to Wagamama. *European Intellectual Property Review,* **17**, 521-525

Copyright as an Economic Incentive

Ruth Towse

Synopsis

This paper pursues the theme set by Mr Justice Laddie and Mr Justice Jacob, which echoes a long-running debate by economists on the economic justification of intellectual property rights. The economic literature on copyright is reviewed. The purpose of copyright is to provide an incentive to authors as creators and to publishers as disseminators of their works via the market mechanism. The underlying assumption is a harmony of interests between author and publisher; each needs the other and as long as the rights and duties of each party are well-defined, their common desire for pecuniary reward provides mutual incentive. Copyright, however, is a bundle of rights which have different financial values; as a consequence, the incentives to the parties alter and so does the bargaining power between them. This leads to principal-agency problems.

The interaction of copyright law and markets in the arts and cultural industries, propelled by technological developments that have both reduced the cost of copying and vastly extended markets, has led to the formation and growth of collecting societies. They are natural monopolies and their operations have added to existing concerns about the statutory monopoly created by copyright law. Their monopoly power is tolerated, however, because they assist the working of the market by collective licensing, besides enabling individuals to secure royalty and other benefits. While that reduces some transaction costs, it also increases others. Ultimately, the economic approach to policy issues such as extensions to copyright (e.g. to performers) is to ask if the extra benefits outweigh the extra costs. We are far from having empirical data on these variables but I have made a start by looking at the distribution of royalties and licence fees by collecting societies as a way of estimating the extent to which copyright law provides a financial incentive to individual artists. The result is not very encouraging - it certainly appears that copyright law is over-rated in this particular respect.

Introduction

Copyright law is a development of market economies. It filled the gap left by the demise of the guild system in Europe which, in conjunction with grants of monopolies, controlled the supply and set the prices of books and works of art. The economic purpose of copyright is to combat market failure from free-riding, thus providing incentives to producers - authors, the primary creators of ideas, and publishers, the disseminators of ideas. Changes to copyright law have been driven by technological innovation resulting in new products - mechanical recording, television, cable and satellite broadcasting, computers and so on - which have enabled authors and publishers to reach huge markets, and in new means of copying - photocopiers, laser printing, home-taping of sound and video recording - which have vastly reduced the cost of making copies and at the same time raised the cost of enforcing copyright. 'Copyright' has become a bundle of diverse rights reflecting product and process innovation as the law accommodates technical changes in what is inevitably a non-stop race. Extensions of the law also embrace changing cultural values and social attitudes to the role of artists, for example, performers.

The international aspects of copyright and its enforcement are a further development during this century, as international trade in copyright material has expanded, multiplying both royalty earnings and the cost of effective enforcement. The market response was the setting up of collecting societies, non-profit membership organisations, to monitor the use of copyright material, collect and distribute royalties and engage in protective measures. From the outset, national societies collaborated through (private) reciprocal agreement to act for foreign authors. At the governmental level, reciprocity has been formalised via international conventions, the Berne and Rome Conventions These culminated recently in the TRIPS Convention of the Uruguay Round of GATT, whose worldwide coverage has significantly increased copyright protection.

The output of copyright-protected industries is growing in all North countries and is beginning to be important as many overseas rights are established and enforced. It has been estimated that in 1993, the 'sector' in the UK accounted for nearly 4% of GDP. The music industry is estimated to contribute £2.5bn to UK GDP; it is also an important source of export earnings having net export earnings of £500m in 1990 (British Invisibles 1995; Dane, Feist and Laing 1996).

Despite the economic importance of copyright, it is a relatively neglected area as far as economists are concerned. While there has been significant work, both theoretical and empirical, on the economics of patents and R&D, copyright has not received so much attention. Yet it is a fruitful area for the application of law and economics and of modern theories of industrial organisation. In addition, the public choice implications of copyright abound. 'Better protection' for authors is widely touted as a motive for changing copyright law worldwide, though publishers, i.e. the firms in cultural industries, almost certainly benefit more and in the past it was they who pressed for the changes. Nowadays those who represent creative and performing artists, their trade unions and professional societies, arts councils and ministers of culture, and international organisations, such as UNESCO, increasingly lobby for the use of copyright law to strengthen the status of artists and their financial bargaining position. Copyright law is gradually coming to be used as regulatory framework for the cultural sector with little understanding of the way markets respond to it. The massive transactions costs that this policy entails have not been estimated. What was in the eighteenth century a device for providing market incentives to book publishing has expanded almost beyond recognition into every office and home. Even the business of collecting royalties has become a booming industry. For all this, copyright, as suspected by authors as early as Milton, has not made many primary creators rich.

The Economic Approach to Copyright

The economic literature on copyright divides fairly neatly into three approaches: early writers, Plant (1934), Hurt and Schuchman (1966) and Breyer (1970) questioned the case for copyright; the focus of their argument was the dynamic incentive copyright provides in stimulating *author's* supply. Later writers such as Novos and Waldman (1984), Johnson (1985) and Landes and Posner (1989) adopted a general welfare approach and developed comparative static models in order to consider the theoretical effect on markets of changes to copyright law; their focus is on the trade-off or balance between the marginal social cost and the marginal social benefit. Landes and Posner, whose analysis of the law and economics of all aspects of intellectual property law has come to be regarded as definitive, not only do not question the case for copyright, they regard the basis of all legal doctrines as being a sort of modern invisible hand that overcomes market failure and promotes private economic efficiency and social welfare. The merit of that approach is that it throws the emphasis on to the relation between the fixed costs of expression (writing the book, making the master tape) and the marginal cost of making copies, whether legal or pirated ones.[1] The drawback is that these models simply assume that incentives to author and publisher work harmoniously and somehow produce the socially desired outcome.

The third approach of economists writing on copyright is to consider the implementation of copyright. There has been some theoretical work, for example, by Smith (1986) and by Besen, Kirkby and Salop (1992) on the economics of copyright collectives but a more interesting aspect of the literature is empirical work by Peacock and Weir (1975), Peacock (1979), MacQueen and Peacock (1995) and Taylor and Towse (1997) that investigates the complex institutional arrangements for the administration of copyright, mainly in the music industry, where collection societies have been established longest. The best source of empirical data on the music industry, however, has come from the Monopolies and Mergers Commission (MMC), gathered during their investigations of monopoly practices on the part of collecting societies and in the record industry (MMC 1988, 1994 and 1996). Policy on copyright, for example, whether to increase its breadth or duration, can and should be decided on the basis of empirical evidence. One issue here is whether the financial rewards to artists (authors, visual artists, composers, etc and performers) from royalty and licence fee income are sufficiently large to provide a real incentive, and I later present some figures gathered in the course of my work on copyright earnings. A subsequent question is whether the 'size' of the incentive balances the costs of implementation, a topic which is tentatively explored in Taylor and Towse (1997). Before that, I go into more detail on the economic analysis of copyright as an incentive.

Copyright as an Economic Incentive

Plant (1934) doubted the need for copyright as an incentive to authors; he believed it to be irrelevant to 'unpaid authors' i.e. academics and the like - the dilettanti - and that 'professional authors' would be, and in the past had been, remunerated via the market. Plant considered but rejected the possible use of state subsidy to a select few authors as an alternative to copyright as an incentive to produce 'great works'. Hurt and Schuchman (1966) took the same line as Plant, however taking a more favourable view than he did of state or private patronage, recommending tax-breaks, grants and prizes as means of providing incentives to authors of worthwhile but 'unpopular' work. Breyer (1970) also preferred a system of subsidies and patronage to copyright as an incentive to authors of works of lasting social value on the grounds that copyright favours popular works with large sales, those that are anyway commercially viable; he pointed out that higher prices resulting from copyright would be particularly harmful to the dissemination of great works. The question of the value of the direct incentives copyright offers authors, then, is whether it results in the output of sub-marginal works and whether it is better at doing so than a system of subsidy and patronage. Both impose costs on society, though the distribution of costs would be different, unless taxpayers have similar patterns of cultural consumption.

The stronger case for copyright is that it also offers incentives to authors indirectly by giving incentives to publishers, who contract with authors. This view, however, assumes a harmony of interests between author and publisher, one that some economists appear to support but others have disputed.

The incentive offered to publishers by the temporary monopoly copyright allows is 'lead time' in which to recoup their fixed costs. It therefore reduces risk. Copiers free-ride on 'first' publishers by avoiding set-up costs, most advertising costs, royalty payments to authors and the risk of failure. In principle, the optimal duration of copyright protection would be a period just long enough to enable publishers to make a normal return on their outlays on each work. In practice, it is uniform and does not distinguish between works which find a ready market and those that take several generations to cover costs. Plant, Hurt and Schuchman and Breyer all believed that copyright protection lasted too long; the first publisher's lead time alone, arising from his inventive entrepreneurship, gave him sufficient advantage in the market and so copyright protection is an unnecessary incentive; Breyer, the only one to have attempted to produce empirical evidence, 'proved' that copyright lasted too long by showing that only a very small percentage of books in copyright were still in print.

Plant viewed copyright, in modern parlance, as the result of rent-seeking by publishers, who exaggerate the riskiness of their enterprise; monopoly protection, by reducing the risk of the first publisher, promoted *over*-production of books (he only considered book publishing); it resulted in too many publishers, too many books and the publication of inferior literature, since it drew in sub-marginal producers, all at prices that were too high. (Hurt and Schuchman, while avoiding Plant's value judgement on quality, pointed out that copyright only has social benefits if it does bring sub-marginal books into production; otherwise, it merely confers economic rent on those that would anyway be profitable.)

Plant advocated a policy of gradual withdrawal of copyright protection; authors would retain their entitlement to royalties but publishers would be restricted to a five-year monopoly (five years after first publication of a work), with both subject to compulsory licences. His proposal therefore offered a compromise between having no copyright system and over-long protection by giving the first publisher a reasonable headstart but throwing the work on the market thereafter.

Undoubtedly, the lead-time advantage of the first publisher has been considerably reduced by technical progress in the years since these articles were published, as copying has become easier and cheaper. However, it may also be the case that cultural products (books, records, films, etc) have a shorter shelf-life than they did in the past. If copyrights were more like patents, as Plant advocated they should be, renewals would act as some sort of guide to the value of the copyright to authors and publishers. Breyer's attempt at testing the value of copyright suggests an approach that could be applied to a whole range of cultural goods. Again, how long copyright protection is needed to promote the production of different goods is an empirical question. We already have a crude differential in fifty years for records, films etc and seventy years for books but one could surely ask why not five years for pop music records and twenty-five for classical records? (See MacQueen and Peacock 1995: 159 for discussion of this issue).

Incentives and Principal-Agency Issues

Plant disputed the harmony of interest between author and publisher. In terms now familiar to every first year student of economics, he pointed out, as an instance of conflict, that the incentive to authors is achieved at the sales maximising price and output where royalties are maximised, whereas the publisher sets a profit maximising price and output. There is thus a conflict of interest (in the absence of joint entrepreneurship) between the two, a point that later writers have ignored. This conflict raises the question of agency. Who is the principal and who is the agent - author or publisher? Are their actions (of the one or the other) such as to justify having even the temporary monopoly society has conferred on them? These questions are obviously relevant to the effectiveness of copyright as an incentive. When there is divergence between the interests of author and publisher (and the number of court cases demonstrates there is, the George Michael case being a recent one [see *Panayiotou v Sony Music Entertainment (UK) Ltd* [1994] EMLR 229]), principal-agent problems arise.

There are, so to speak, two levels at which principal-agency issues exist; at the societal level and at the individual level. As a society, we wish to promote creativity and the dissemination of ideas and do so by means of establishing intellectual property rights that provide market incentives to advance those ends. If author and publisher had identical interests, it would be plain sailing. But authors and publishers do not bargain equally and there are asymmetries. Publishers by and large have better access to capital markets and greater economic power than authors, who are typically more numerous and in strong competition with each other to get their work published.[2] There are economies of scale in publishing though not in authorship. We are forced therefore to rely heavily on publishers (often huge, unregulated conglomerates) to select those works we wish to see published, while having little control over the outcome. One has only to think of social concern over the content of TV programmes, films and videos to get the point.

The application of principal-agency analysis to the royalty system of payment is an unexplored area of the economics of copyright and produces useful insights about the effectiveness of economic incentives to authors. The royalty system causes author and publisher to share risk. There are three basic possibilities:

- risk is equally shared in a joint entrepreneurship (which would harmonise the two parties' interests);
- risk is shared unequally between author and publisher;
- the author avoids risk completely by doing a "buy-out" deal, that is selling her rights to the publisher for a lump sum.

Joint entrepreneurship is rare but something along those lines occurs with top pop and film stars; the Beatles' Apple Corporation is an instance. Top pop groups get large advances from their record company which they use to finance the making of their next album; they take charge of all the arrangements for recording - hiring sound engineers, record producers, studios, backing performers, video producers, even artists to design album jackets, etc. The record company's task is promotion and marketing. Film stars may similarly share control of their films. Such stars are often wealthy enough to finance their own operations but apparently choose not to do so.

Risk may be shared between author and publisher in various degrees. When the author has a good bargaining position, by virtue of reputation and/or talent, the publisher attempts to secure her services by means of an exclusive contract and a lump sum advance on future royalty payments. The higher the advance, the greater the share of risk the publisher accepts, and the greater is his incentive to market the work and exploit the rights assigned to him. Because quality is usually an important feature, contracts are incomplete (even though they run to hundreds of pages!) and there are moral hazard problems.[3] By contrast, an unknown author gets no advance and may only be paid royalties after so many copies are sold; the publisher bears little of the risk and the author's problem is to get him to market her work satisfactorily.

The total buy-out deal is where the author avoids risk by taking an up-front payment in exchange for all rights. Considering why buy-outs are regarded as undesirable by authors and performers provides some insight into the economic rationale for risk-sharing deals. Later we discuss the fact that new copyright regulations implementing the EC Rental Directive make some rights unwaivable i.e. they specifically seek to prevent buy-outs.[4]

Buy-outs occur when the author (often a performer) has no reputation or distinguishing talent that is sought by the publisher. Typical examples are backing artists in sound recordings, walk-on part actors and extras in films. These are people who, it is argued, may be easily exploited because of low bargaining power. Buy-outs are favoured by publishers because they reduce transaction costs; the publisher bears all the risk and is free to use all rights in the work.[5] If authors or performers were indifferent to risk and there were no uncertainty, they should be indifferent as between a lump sum representing the present value of all future income and that same stream paid out annually over fifty or seventy years.[6] Most authors are reluctant to agree to buy-outs and their trade unions and professional associations advise against them (except in a few circumstances), regarding them with deep suspicion. As many 'jobbing' musicians and actors work on standard contracts agreed by Equity (the actors' union) and the Musicians' Union (MU) with the various industry representatives, royalties rather than buy-outs are the norm, i.e. risk is shared between performer and producer.[7] Even so, many performers do occasional jobs on the 'black market' for a buy-out.

Suspicion of buy-outs is based on asymmetries of information about risk as between author (performer) and publisher (record company). Publishers are regarded as having better information about future technology and the scope of market exploitation which they are not trusted to disclose to authors. In addition (though this has nothing to do with risk per se), they do not trust them to pass on correct information about revenue which is to be shared. Other asymmetries may exist; author and publisher may have different attitudes to risk and to time preference. Only if an author has an unusually strong bequest motive (to her grandchildren) would the extension of copyright from 50 to 70 years provide any change in incentive; however it could be significant to a publishing firm, whose assets are a portfolio of rights.

But there is a further and more subtle objection to buy-outs, at least for 'named' artists i.e. those with individual contracts with the publisher: as their reputation increases, the demand for their early work rises. Without a residual claim to a share in the increased value they have created, that increase in value would accrue solely to the publisher. That is when their subsequent output is complementary. It could also be a substitute, though: most people prefer earlier to later Callas recordings; thus Callas in 1965 competed with Callas in 1950. Either way, a buy-out would reduce the artist's share of revenue from her own reputation. Although it could be argued that there are losers as well as winners, most artists have an unshakeable belief in their abilities - Adam Smith's 'overweening conceit'- and so prefer to retain a claim to future income which means accepting a share of risk.

Enough has been said to show that we must drop the assumption of harmony of interests between author and publisher. The effect of conflict distorts incentives and opens the way for rent-seeking pressure on governments to 'regulate' the cultural industries via the copyright system.

Collecting Societies and Transaction Costs

The bundle of rights we commonly refer to as copyright is exploited and administered in a complex system that has spontaneously developed for the collection and distribution of royalties and to license and monitor use. In what may be called the primary market - sales of books, records etc. - royalties are relatively simple to administer; the publisher pays the agreed percentage of sales revenue direct to the author and bears the (small) administrative cost. But in secondary markets, such as broadcast of sound recordings, films reformatted as videos, cable retransmission of TV programmes, photocopying and suchlike, contact between copyright-holder and user is severed. Rights are then administered by collecting societies. In order to analyse the operations of the collecting societies, it is necessary to go into some detail. The UK music business is a good example.

In the UK, collecting societies perform three functions with respect to (a) specific right(s):

- they collect royalties and fees from the licences they sell for secondary uses
- they monitor uses (and prosecute infringers);
- they distribute revenues to UK members and transfer to equivalent foreign societies that share of receipts due to foreign authors.

They are open membership societies which act on behalf of copyright-holders, both authors and publishers, as assignees or agents for a specific right or group of rights. The member transfers that right for all her works to the society for exploitation. That is mostly done by the sale of blanket licences to users, which entitle them to use every member's works. There are twenty such societies in the UK, each having a monopoly for specific rights. Thus, for instance, Phonographic Performance Ltd (PPL), the collecting society for record companies, administers the public performance right in sound recording by selling licences to firms which play recorded music (radio and TV stations, shops, restaurants, hotels and aeroplanes, to give only a few examples of secondary use); the firm, which would otherwise have to transact individually with each record company whose music they wanted to play, gains access to the whole repertoire. PPL then distributes fees, after deducting administrative costs, to the record companies, named artists and backing artists according to estimated audience size and frequency of use (see below and MMC (1988) for further details). Radio and TV broadcasters log the number of times a week a recording is played and make a return to PPL. Firms have to go through the same process with the Performing Right Society in order to pay composers' royalties. The underlying rationale for setting tariffs is the pay-for-play principle, that final consumers 'pay' for their consumption of musical performances (see MacQueen and Peacock (1995) and Taylor and Towse (1997)).

Collecting societies are natural monopolies for the rights they administer. There are two chief benefits: they enable different rights-owners to be remunerated for all uses of their rights by having access to a network of collection and monitoring arrangements which pool costs (which would otherwise be prohibitive for all but very high-earning stars); and they provide a simplified service to firms, a one-stop-shop, through blanket licensing. They thus reduce transactions costs for copyright-owners and licensees. These benefits must be balanced against the monopoly pricing of licences and monopoly 'pricing' of administration charges, since the monopoly also means that rightsholders are forced to use the services of one organisation. The Monopolies and Mergers Commission report on the Performing Rights Society (PRS) expressed concern about internal administrative efficiency as PRS charges its members over 17% for administering performing rights.[8] This, however, is low in contrast to deductions for administration in other countries; in Italy, the equivalent to PRS deducts nearly 60% (MMC, 1996).

The basis on which royalties and licence revenues are distributed by the collecting society has been a source of considerable internal friction between members in the case of the PRS. Collecting societies have to balance their administrative costs and their members' interests in obtaining the remuneration due to them. Cross-subsidisation may therefore occur for reasons of cost-saving. It may also be the favoured policy; for example in the PRS, classical composers are cross-subsidised by pop composers (MMC 1996). The collective exercise of rights, therefore, inevitably blunts individual incentive; for it to be otherwise would require a more finely-tuned and hence more costly administrative set-up.

The division of revenue at PPL has also caused problems over the years; until 1996, it distributed 67.5% of its net income to the record company, 20% to the named artists and 12.5% to backing performers. With the recent introduction of the new performer's right to equitable remuneration for sound recording, this division has been voluntarily changed to a 50:50 split between (all) performers and the record companies. Performers' representatives, however, claim that without a statutory right to a half share and no power to influence the setting of licence fees, inspecting accounts, and the like, they can do better setting up their own collection society for this right. That, however, is likely to duplicate collection costs (see Taylor and Towse 1997). This is further evidence of conflict of interest between 'partners in copyright' and of lack of trust.

To sum up, then. Economic analysis of copyright must take account of the way it is implemented. Collection societies are the established mode of collecting and distributing remuneration for members and for exploiting rights. They are regarded as desirable by lawmakers and the MMC. However, they introduce a new dimension to the structure of incentives to authors and publishers.

Policy Issues

Significant changes have recently been made to copyright law in the UK. EC Directives on Rental and Lending Rights, the Duration of Copyright and on

COPYRIGHT AS AN ECONOMIC INCENTIVE 41

Satellite Broadcasts and Cable Retransmissions have extended the scope and duration of copyright. Performers have been given new rights, the right to equitable remuneration from the exploitation of sound recordings by broadcasts and other means, and new property rights in rental and lending, reproduction and distribution. I shall concentrate here mostly on the performer's right to equitable remuneration from sound recording.

That right has been made unwaivable by the Rental Directive and, according to the UK statutory instrument, the Copyright and Related Rights Regulations 1996/2967 adopted in 1996, may only be assigned to a collecting society whose objective is the collection of performers' remuneration. The Performing Artists' Media Rights Association (PAMRA) has been set up with that purpose. The right is an individual one and therefore every performer's contribution to every track of every sound recording must be logged and revenues apportioned accordingly for full compliance. One method of 'total' logging is to have an internationally agreed encryption system (the ISRC - an example, by the way, of how technological advances assist monitoring of use); that will add to the costs of record production and could conceivably raise the price of records on sale to the public as well as imposing costs on licensees. Whatever system is adopted for tracing and collecting for every individual seems certain to raise transactions costs (see Taylor and Towse 1997 for details).[9]

Pressure for these changes has come from organisations representing performers, who, like other artists, see copyright law as an instrument for improving their bargaining position. They believe, it seems, that any extension of copyright is bound to result in higher remuneration and fail to understand that markets discount any future claims to revenues. Moreover, they are backed up by Arts Councils and the like, who see copyright as a (to them) costless way of satisfying artists' demands; it is cheaper than subsidy and they do not have to bear any resulting costs! In the past, however, it was the publishers who were the active rent-seekers, as Plant noted; even before the Statute of Anne, authors, including Defoe, Pope and Dryden, resisted the introduction of copyright! (See Rose 1993). Thus copyright law has long been a forum for rent-seeking activity due to economic conflicts between author and publisher. One outcome is that changes to the law can cause higher transactions costs without raising incentives. That may well be the case with the new performers' right in sound recording. Making the right unwaivable represents a significant change of approach to copyright law in the UK, which by and large facilitates all means of exploiting rights. Indeed, one could go further and see this more as an instance of an incipient tendency to use copyright law to regulate the music market.

The Value of Copyright Earnings

Finally, I present some empirical evidence on the financial value of copyright to authors, mainly musicians (composers and performers). In a recent paper (Towse 1997), I assembled data on the distribution by collecting societies of royalties and licence fee income to their members. The total sums are quite large: for example, the Performing Rights Society distributed £128.5m in 1993; £20.4m to authors, £31.1m to publishers and £24m to affiliated foreign societies. The distribution to individual writers (authors), however, is extremely skewed, showing how little the majority earn from rights in performance, though a few earn a great deal:

> 31% received under £25.
> 22% received £25-99.
> Altogether, 90 per cent of PRS writers received less than £1,000 in 1993.

The Mechanical Copyright Protection Society (MCPS) distributed £114.6m in 1994 to composers and music publishers. Details of the distribution to individual composers are not published, but it seems likely to be similar to that of PRS.

Phonographic Performance Ltd (PPL) distributed £30.6m from licensing public performances of sound recordings in 1994. It distributed £21.2m to record companies and £9.4m to performers. The 12.5% share for the backing artists, an amount of approximately £3m shared between 9,000 or so individuals, was distributed via the Musicians' Union for the years 1989-1995; the typical (median) musician received £75 a year averaged over that period.

Though these totals add up to £274m, it is clear that composers and musicians *typically* earn peanuts from their rights in performance. A few top stars earn very significant sums; even among the backing musicians, ten earned over £30,000 each over the six years. But the vast majority earn so little it barely covers the cost of registering their works with a collecting society and certainly cannot be said to provide even a marginal financial incentive to compose or perform. That is not the whole story because musicians are paid for the recording session by the record company; the current rate for a three-hour call is £90.[10] A good 'sessions' player could expect to make £20,000-£50,000 a year from session fees. But that figure obviously dwarfs the royalties from secondary usage for which the new performers' rights were created.

It might well be argued that these are early days for performers' rights, and that these figures are unrepresentative. Against that claim, data from similar activities in Sweden and Denmark, which adopted the Rome Convention a decade ago, show exactly the same pattern of performers' earnings as the PPL distribution. The protagonists also point to the fact that secondary use (in broadcasting, cable transmission, pubs, ships, aircraft etc) is growing and the figures show that income from public performance licences has increased considerably; for example PRS' gross income rose from £74m in 1985 to £179m in 1995). The size of the cake has undoubtedly increased in real terms and with it the size of the slices. Nevertheless, they fall far short of providing a livelihood and do not "allow authors, musicians and the like to support themselves by their creative efforts", the phrase used by Mr Justice Laddie. In this respect, too, he was correct in viewing copyright as 'overrated' (see above).

Conclusion

What Mr Justice Laddie described as a balancing act would be characterised by economists as a trade-off. The standard welfare view, such as that of Landes and Posner, is that the marginal benefit of broadening the law of copyright must be balanced or traded off against the increased marginal cost. The benefit is the incentive to authors and performers; the traditional view of the marginal cost is the reduction in access either to consumers via the effect of higher prices (Plant, Hurt and Schuchman, Johnson, Novos and Waldman), or to producers via the reduction of the number of works in the public domain (Landes and Posner). It has been argued here that two other factors merit some attention; transaction costs and the riskiness or even uncertainty in the markets for goods and services that are inherently novel. Much more work has to be done on the economic effects of changes in copyright law, such as the introduction of performers' rights, on transaction costs, not just those of the collecting societies but also indirect costs passed on to other authors, producers and consumers. There is also much to be done on the economic analysis of the role of economic risk and uncertainty in the system of incentives that copyright law seeks to provide. Above all, we need more empirical evidence on individuals' earnings from copyright. The little provided here is just a start. Only when we have more evidence will it be possible to judge how economically efficient copyright law is as an incentive to creative activity.

* * * * *

This paper is based on work undertaken during the project "Copyright, Performers' Rights and Incentives in Cultural Markets" funded by the Economic and Social Research Council (L126251011).

Notes

1   O'Hare (1985) considers this relationship in different art forms, making an interesting case for different duration of protection.
2   Word has it that well-known publishers of fiction are sent 200-300 unsolicited manuscripts a week. The small number of cases where previously unknown authors succeed in getting published this way are widely reported precisely because it is so unusual. What happens to the vast majority of the unsuccessful - in every branch of the arts - is never documented. There appears to be excess supply in every art form: see Towse (1996).
3   Recent examples of the problem are the case against Joan Collins and the book by Naomi Campbell. Moral hazard occurs when the principal's incentive attracts the wrong agent!
4   See Reinbothe and von Lewinski (1993 : 66).
5   This is becoming an important issue in cable retransmission of TV programmes. According to an article by Meg Carter in *The Independent*

24 September 1996, UK Gold had to send out over 1,000 letters to clear 'The Sweeney' and 'Minder' for cable broadcast. There are now firms that specialise in clearing TV and other such rights for secondary use.

6 That markets discount claims on future earnings has been demonstrated in relation to artists' resale rights (*droit de suite*). The price of works of art falls when a percentage of the increase in value has to be paid on resale, another unwaivable right to be introduced by EC Directive (Ginsburgh 1996 and Jacob 1997). In principle the extension of the duration of copyright for authors from fifty to seventy years also reduces the present value of a work; however, discounting so far into the future makes little numerical difference. A reduction of the duration of copyright, say to twenty years pma would certainly raise the up-front (spot) price. A point that is rarely made about *droit de suite* is that artists are not charged a fee by those who purchased their works when resale prices fall. Such a scheme might demonstrate there are more losers then winners!

7 In fact, the situation is a great deal more complicated but this is not the place to go into detail. A couple of examples are useful here, however. Actors used to receive residual payments and repeat fees for retransmissions of TV programmes; that has now changed to a royalty. (This has nothing to do with the new performers' rights; it was done to allow cable exploitation.) The Musicians' Union has agreed with the BBC for a buy-out of the BBC orchestras' musicians rights in some TV programmes. The fee that backing musicians are paid for recording sessions includes a buy-out for the rights from the sale of records.

8 The figure for domestic licensing revenue was 26% in 1994. PRS royalty revenue was £163m and its administration expenses over £28m (MMC 1996 : 76, 80).

9 Mechanical rights collection societies are at present merging their data bases and licensing arrangements, a move that is expected to reduce administrative costs. Better use of IT could eventually lead to mergers between societies across Europe, even worldwide. Transaction costs would be reduced to the rightsholders at the potential cost of greater monopoly power in setting licence fees to users.

10 That figure includes the buy-out on record sales - see note 7 above.

Bibliography

Besen, S., Kirkby, S., and Salop, S., (1992). An economic analysis of copyright collectives, *Virginia Law Review*, **78**, 383-411.

Besen, S., and Raskind, L., (1991). An introduction to the law and economics of intellectual property, *Journal of Economic Perspectives*, **5**,1; 3-27.

Breyer, S., (1970). The uneasy case for copyright, *Harvard Law Review*, **84**; 281-351.

Dane, C., Feist, A., and Laing, D., (1996). *The Value of Music.* London, National Music Council.

Hurt, R., and Schuchman, R., (1966). The economic rationale of copyright. *American Economic Review*, **56**; 421-432.

Ginsburgh, V., (1996). On the economic consequences of resale rights on art. *The Art Newspaper,* **59**, May; 1-11.

Jacob, R., (1997). Industrial property - industry's enemy? *Intellectual Property Quarterly*, **1**, 3-15.

Johnson, W., (1985). The economics of copyright, *Journal of Political Economy*, **93**, 1; 158-174.

Laddie, H., (1996). Copyright: over-strength, over-regulated, over-rated? *European Intellectual Property Review*, **17**, 253-260.

Landes, W., and Posner, R., (1989). An economic analysis of copyright law, *Journal of Legal Studies*, **18**; 325-366.

MacQueen, H.L., and Peacock, A.T., (1995). Implementing performance rights, *Journal of Cultural Economics*, **19**,2; 147-175.

Monopolies and Mergers Commission (1988). *Collective Licensing.* HMSO Cm 550, London.

Monopolies and Mergers Commission (1994). *The Supply of Recorded Music.* HMSO Cm 2599, London.

Monopolies and Mergers Commission (1996). *Performing Rights*, HMSO Cm 3147, London.

Novos, I., and Waldman, M., (1984). The effects of increased copyright protection, *Journal of Political Economy*, 92,2; 236—46.

O'Hare, M., (1985). Copyright: when is monopoly efficient? *Journal of Policy Analysis and Management* , 4,3: 407-418.

Peacock, A.T., (1979). Public policy and copyright in music: An economic analysis. In *The Economic Analysis of Government*. Martin Robertson : Oxford.

Peacock, A.T., and Weir, R., (1975). *The Composer in the Marketplace*. Faber : London.

Plant, A., (1934). The economic aspects of copyright in books. *Economica*, May: 167-195

Price, T., (1993). *The Economic Importance of Copyright.* Common Law Institute of Intellectual Property, London.

Reinbothe, J., and von Lewinski, S., (1993). *The EC Directive on Rental and Lending Rights and on Piracy.* Sweet and Maxwell : London.

Rose, M., (1993). *Authors and Owners : The Invention of Copyright*. Harvard University Press : Cambridge/London.

Smith, D., (1986). Collective administration of copyright, in Palmers, J., (ed), *Research in Law and Economics*, **8**; 137-151.

Taylor, M., and Towse, R., (1997). *The Value of Performers' Rights: An Economic Approach*. University of Exeter, mimeo.

Towse, R., (1996). Economics of training artists, in Ginsburgh, V., and Menger, P-M., (eds), *Economics of the Arts*, North Holland, Amsterdam; 303-329.

Towse, R., (1997). Artists' earnings from copyright and related rights. Paper presented at Workshop on the Economics of Artists and Art Policy, Helsinki, University of Exeter, mimeo.

Biotechnology : Facing the Problems of Patent Law

Graeme T Laurie

Synopsis

This paper examines the problems which biotechnology companies have encountered in seeking patent protection for the fruits of their labour in the United Kingdom and Europe. In stark contrast to the United States, the courts of the United Kingdom have adopted a relatively hostile stance towards biotechnology inventions, and in the European Patent Office the issue of the morality of patenting 'life' has led to a state of confusion and uncertainty in European patent law. These problems have conspired to make Europe a singularly unattractive option for biotechnology investors and to weaken Europe's economic standing in a field which is set to dominate the technologies of the twenty first century. This paper argues that certainty and stability can come to European patent law through amendment of the European Patent Convention to reflect a strong economic policy that biotechnological inventions are to be encouraged and protected to the same extent as in the United States. The question of morality in essence concerns the act of creation and not that of protection, and as such is misplaced and ineffective within the patent system.

Introduction

Ever since humanity has organised itself into social and cultural groups it has manipulated the genetic material of living organisms through haphazard selection and cross-breeding. Since the 1970s, however, the science of biotechnology has resulted in the *direct* manipulation of genetic material at the cellular and sub-cellular level. Because this can be done with a high degree of accuracy, the results can be predicted with more certainty than "traditional" techniques. The benefits which this science offers are astounding. In the health sphere biotechnological advances have given rise to the development of test kits, medical treatments and new drugs. In farming, agriculture and horticulture genetic manipulation can produce more robust varieties of animals and plants than traditional methods, and genetic alteration of food holds the promise of bigger, better tasting and longer lasting produce on supermarket shelves. Indeed, the idea that there is nothing we cannot bring under our control was seemingly vindicated in February 1997 when the Roslin Institute in Edinburgh offered to the world "Dolly" the sheep - the first creature ever to be cloned from adult cells (Wilmut *et al*, 1997). This is not to suggest, however, that the advent of biotechnology has been free of moral opprobrium. Indeed, quite the opposite is true, and much disquiet has been expressed about the work of the biotechnology industry, particularly on the issue of patenting biotechnological inventions. In the USA a favourable approach has been adopted towards the biotechnology industry in the name of economic development, but in Europe and the United Kingdom different policy considerations have placed considerable obstacles in the path of prospective biotechnology patentees. In part, this has contributed to the considerable differences which exist between the standing of biotechnology in Europe compared to the USA.

In financial terms the biotechnology industry has enormous earning potential. European revenues in 1996 exceeded 1,700 million Ecu. In the period between 1995 and 1996 the number of European biotechnology companies grew by 23% to over 700, employing some 27,500 people. In the USA, however, over 1,300 companies employ almost 120,000. In 1996 revenue exceeded 11,600 million Ecu (Ernst & Young, 1997). This shows clearly that the European biotechnology industry is still relatively small compared to that in the USA, and although European growth is fast at the present time, these figures highlight the need for strong incentives to encourage biotech investment in Europe to facilitate healthy competition with the USA in this lucrative market.

This paper considers matters of policy and morality on three levels. First, it examines the likely future approach of the UK courts towards biotechnological inventions in light of the 1996 House of Lords' decision in *Biogen v Medeva* [1997] RPC 1. Second, it reviews the disharmony of approach towards biotechnology patents (a) as between the United Kingdom and the European Patent Office (EPO) in interpreting European patent law, and (b) as between the EPO and other jurisdictions concerning the role of morality in the grant of a patent. Finally, it assesses whether the introduction of the European Draft Directive on the legal protection of biotechnological inventions can address adequately the economic and moral concerns currently surrounding the patentability of biotechnology.

Biotechnology patents in the United Kingdom

Like all prospective patentees in the UK, the inventor of a biotechnological product or process must satisfy the criteria for patentability contained in section 1(1) of the Patents Act 1977 (henceforth PA 1977). That is, it must be shown that the "invention" is new, that it involves an "inventive step" (in the sense that the invention would not be obvious to someone skilled in the particular field) and that it has industrial applicability (that it can be made or used in any type of industry). Additionally, the invention must not be excluded from patentability on a number of established grounds. For example, it must not be a discovery as such, nor must it be likely to encourage morally or socially offensive behaviour, nor must it relate to animal or plant varieties (PA 1977, s.1(2)(a), 1(3)(a) and (b)).

From the very beginning biotechnology inventors faced problems of patentability in the British courts. The source of these problems stem essentially from the same fact: the work of the industry concerns the manipulation of naturally-occurring "living" organisms and their component parts. To date, only one biotechnology patent has been held to be valid in the superior courts (*Chiron Corp. and Others v Murex Diagnostics and Others; Chiron Corp. and Others v Organ Teknika and Others* [1996] FSR 153).

* * * * *

When the House of Lords came to hear *Biogen v Medeva* it faced several interpretations of patent law from the Court of Appeal which were distinctly unfavourable to the biotechnology industry.

In *Genentech Inc.'s patent* [1989] RPC 147 the plaintiff had produced and patented human tissue plasminogen activator (t-PA), a protein occurring naturally in the human body which assists in dissolving blood clots. Using genetic engineering techniques (recombinant DNA technology) Genentech was able to produce sufficient quantities of t-PA in a pure enough form to market as a therapeutic agent. At least five other teams embarked on similar work at considerable expense and with a degree of uncertainty of success. The Court of Appeal held that because the dispute related to naturally occurring substances the plaintiffs had to demonstrate an "invention" *in addition* to satisfying the criteria for patentability of novelty, inventive step and industrial applicability (at 263 - 264). The court stated that it was not an "invention" to manufacture an "existing substance" with known properties by the application of known technology (at 259). This, however, ignored the fact that the substances produced by Genentech do not occur naturally. The t-PA protein came from molecules with a genetic structure which is not that of DNA, but of cDNA (complementary DNA). Importantly, cDNA does not contain "introns" which are sections of DNA which do not "code" for proteins, and it allows the "expression" of the t-PA protein free of other proteins, and hence in a much purer form than is found in nature. For the court to ignore this and to require the additional criterion of "invention" had clear implications for the biotechnology industry which exists to manipulate "naturally occurring" organisms.

In determining obviousness, the Court of Appeal focused on the result obtained rather than on the laborious means used to reach it. What was held to be obvious was the application of known techniques to a known goal. Yet, it was by no means an easy thing to establish the DNA sequence for t-PA, and much time and money had been spent in achieving that goal. This, however, was irrelevant for the court. Moreover, the court's attitude to the hurdles which had to be overcome was to impute to the notional person skilled in the art a degree of inventiveness. As Mustill LJ said:

[w]here the art by its nature involves intellectual gifts and ingenuity of approach, it would, I believe, be wrong to assume that the hypothetical worker is devoid of those gifts. (at 280)

This decision seemed to set a higher standard of test of obviousness for "hi-tech" industries such as the biotechnology industry. Obviousness is normally tested by asking what would have been obvious to a skilled person at the relevant date (priority date) considering the state of the art as it stood and the problem to be solved. The authorities state that such a person is skilled but *unimaginative* (see, for example, *Windsurfing International v Tabur Marine* [1985] RPC 59, which was not referred to by the court in *Genentech*). However, the Court of Appeal held that it was obvious to a skilled person that t-PA could be produced using costly genetic engineering techniques even although success was by no means guaranteed. Furthermore, the skilled "person" in such a hi-tech industry could be a team working towards a particular goal and the team could be held to possess a degree of ingenuity and inventiveness. Indeed, the court opined that this must be so for otherwise they would not be part of the industry at all.

On one view, it is trite that the notional skilled person should assume the traits of those working in the field in question. Unfortunately, the application of this in practice leads to a paradox: those who make considerable advances in the name of benefiting humanity in a field such as biotechnology, and who spend considerable sums in the process, are less likely to be rewarded by the grant of a patent in recognition of their endeavour and as a means of recouping outlays. This means that problems which are encountered on the route to the end goal are more likely to be seen as everyday distractions and therefore less likely to exhibit inventiveness in their resolution. The message given by the Court of Appeal in *Genentech* was that the British courts would do the biotechnology industry no special favours.

In *Biogen v Medeva* [1995] RPC 25; [1995] FSR 4 the Court of Appeal took a similar line, holding that an "invention" was indeed required, and that what the plaintiffs had done was "obvious to try". The patent in question related to Hepatitis B (HBV) and recombinant DNA molecules were claimed which displayed HBV antigen specificity for two different types of HBV antigen (core and surface). The molecules had been produced using genetic engineering techniques when the sequences coding for the antigens were unknown. To a large extent the problem was the same as that which faced Genentech. Biogen had been the only company to proceed along this path, since others considered that the chances of success were very remote indeed. The patent in suit was a European patent lodged in 1979 which claimed priority from an earlier UK patent (Biogen 1 - 22 December 1978). This was necessary because the sequence coding for the HBV antigens was discovered after the 1978 application but before the 1979 application, thereby rendering the latter "obvious". This was accepted by the plaintiffs. In infringement proceedings Aldous J upheld the validity of the patent at first instance but this was overturned by the Court of Appeal. The court took the view that what Biogen had done was "obvious to try" because once Biogen had taken

50 INNOVATION, INCENTIVE AND REWARD

the business decision to embark on the course of applying existing genetic engineering techniques to isolate and express the proteins, everything which followed was obvious. Once again, as with *Genentech*, the Court of Appeal had thwarted the efforts of biotechnology inventors. The court's choice of obviousness test - obvious to try - made it particularly difficult to see how future inventors in the field could secure patent protection. It seemed that it would always be obvious to try to apply genetic engineering techniques to isolate and manipulate the genetic material of living organisms.

In the House of Lords the unanimous decision of the court was delivered by Lord Hoffmann (*Biogen v Medeva* [1997] RPC 1). His approach to the questions of invention, obviousness and priority are dealt with below.

Invention

Lord Hoffmann was unconvinced by the argument that "invention" must be shown. He noted that the drafters of the European Patent Convention (EPC) - implemented in the UK by the PA 1977 "as nearly as practicable" in its entirety - saw no need to define "invention", since in practice to satisfy the four criteria of patentability *is* to produce an "invention". He accepted that in the future it might be possible for a novel creation to satisfy all four criteria and yet not be properly describable as an "invention", but he noted that neither the draftsmen of the EPC, nor those who drew up the PA 1977, nor indeed counsel for the defendants could offer a single example of such a creation. Given this, he was content to cross the bridge should he ever come to it, and determined that for the time being it was sufficient for prospective patentees simply to meet the criteria for patentability contained in section 1(1).

This is welcome. To rule otherwise makes a special case of biotechnological inventions and introduces a wide degree of discretion to the courts to exclude matter from patentability on potentially arbitrary grounds. Lord Mustill reserved judgement on the point (at 31 - 32) and argued that in the future the courts may be required to review the matter, but Lord Hoffmann's response to this is correct: section 1(5) of the 1977 Act allows the Secretary of State to exclude from patentability new creations by laying an order before both Houses of Parliament. This is surely preferable to the haphazard introduction of an indistinct and undefined requirement for "invention". It also displays a degree of confidence on the part of the court in the inherent potential patentability of biotechnological inventions.

Obviousness

Lord Hoffmann took issue with the Court of Appeal's decision on obviousness on three grounds. First, he considered that the reference to commercial gamble was irrelevant:

[t]he fact that a given experimental strategy was adopted for commercial reasons,

because the anticipated rewards seemed to justify the necessary expenditure, is no reason why that strategy should not involve an inventive step. (at 44)

This must be correct. In the same way that considerable expenditure is irrelevant to the question of patentability, so too the willingness to take financial risk should have absolutely no bearing on the determination of inventiveness.

Second, Lord Hoffmann endorsed the *Windsurfing* test for obviousness which had been ignored by the Court of Appeal both in the present case and in *Genentech*. This requires the court to identify the "inventive concept" involved, to impute to the notionally skilled person the current state of the art, to identify the differences between what was invented and what was known, and to ask whether there was an obvious step taken from what was known to what was invented. Applying this, Lord Hoffmann considered that the Court of Appeal was wrong to adopt without question the view of Aldous J. on the "inventive concept". Aldous J. had held that the inventive concept was "the idea or decision to express a polypeptide displaying HBV antigen specificity in a suitable host" (at 45). The Court of Appeal agreed and held that this was simply a choice to pursue an identified goal by known means. Lord Hoffmann also agreed that, *so stated*, the concept was obvious. However, he opted for a different view of the inventive concept. He saw it as, "the idea of trying to express unsequenced eukaryotic DNA in a prokaryotic host" (at 45). Expressed this way, he was prepared to accept that what had been done in 1978 was not obvious.

This is a classic example of judicial activism at work. Although the nature of what had been done was clearly a constant, the way in which it was described and interpreted led different courts to different conclusions. The House of Lords may be demonstrating here a shift in favour of biotechnological patents. Certainly, the courts have it within their power to adopt favourable interpretations of patent law to protect biotechnological inventions, as in the United States (see, for example, *In re Deuel* 34 USPQ 2d 1210 (Fed. Cir. 1995)). All that is needed is a willingness to do so.

Third, Lord Hoffmann opined that an appellate court should rarely question a trial judge's ruling on obviousness, this being "a kind of jury question" (at 45). In light of this he said that he was "content to assume, without deciding, that what [had been done] was not obvious" (at 46). Yet, because he did not rule on the question we are left to wonder what the proper test for assessing obviousness is to be in such cases. We saw that the Court of Appeal applied an 'obvious to try' test, and it did this following the trial judge's lead ([1995] RPC 25 at 112 - 114). In the absence of an express indication to the contrary it is reasonable to assume, therefore, that the House of Lords has endorsed this test. If this is indeed true, it puts the United Kingdom at odds with the European Patent Office and the United States courts, each of which applies an obviousness test which is more favourable to the biotechnology industry. They ask, was the course of conduct used obvious to try *with a reasonable likelihood or expectation of success*? This test was used to uphold Biogen's patent before the EPO (*BIOGEN/Hepatitis B* [1995] EPOR 1). Most recently in the USA it has also been used to uphold a biotechnology patent for retrieved DNA sequences encoding for human and bovine growth factors, irrespective of the fact that "traditional" genetic engineering routes had been employed to reach the goal in question (*In re Deuel* 34 USPQ 2d 1210 (Fed. Cir. 1995)).

Arguably, such a test imposes a more objective standpoint on the question of obviousness compared to the "obvious to try" test, because it includes a requirement that one must have a valid basis for believing that one's approach will bring one to a desired goal before that approach will be deemed to be obvious. As a consequence the test is easier to satisfy from the perspective of the prospective patentee and harder to rely on by those who would challenge biotechnology patents.

The obvious to try test, however, confuses knowledge and obviousness. In the Court of Appeal decisions in *Genentech* and *Biogen* the patents were invalid for obviousness because a known goal was pursued with known techniques. In each case, however, the court ignored the considerable hurdles which had to be overcome, hurdles which would clearly be of relevance if an assessment of the likelihood of success was part of the equation. As with "inventive concept", the question of which test is to be applied is a matter of policy for the courts.

Priority

On the question of whether Biogen could claim priority for its invention from Biogen 1, Lord Hoffmann held that an earlier application can only "support" a later patent application if the former contained an "enabling disclosure" in respect of the invention. That is, the earlier patent application must contain sufficient detail and description of the invention later claimed to allow a person skilled in the particular field to reproduce that invention. Did, therefore, Biogen 1 contain an enabling disclosure in respect of the European patent? Lord Hoffmann held that it did not. The European patent contained very wide claims for (effectively) *all* proteins made by *any* recombinant DNA techniques which display HBV antigen specificity. Thus, the monopoly, if granted, would cover *any* such protein produced from HBV, by *any* genetic engineering technique (existing or yet to be discovered) and irrespective of the host cells used to express the protein (bacterial, mammal or otherwise). What Biogen 1 disclosed (at best) was a means of crudely cutting up the DNA of hepatitis B and expressing certain kinds of proteins with certain kinds of antigen specificity in simple host cells. On this basis Lord Hoffmann held that the claimed invention was excessively broad. It was stated that that which is disclosed must enable the invention to be worked *to the full extent* of the monopoly claimed. Moreover, it was confirmed that monopolies will be awarded for inventions *only* to the extent that the inventions contribute to the state of the art.

In the case of *Biogen* the technical contribution was a way of working with HBV to produce recombinant molecules which had antigen specificity *in the absence* of knowledge about the make-up of the base sequences. However, Lord Hoffmann was emphatic in holding that if there are available ways of achieving the same result without relying on the invention (and therefore without relying on its contribution to the state of the art) then those ways fall outside the monopoly which can legitimately be claimed by the patentee of the invention in question. Here, once the HBV gene sequences were known, it was easy to produce HBV antigens without using Biogen's technique at all.

The problem of overly-broad claims is one which commonly arises whenever a new technology first tries to establish itself within the patent system. Some have even expressed the concern that in the biotechnology industry this was becoming the norm (Crespi 1995: 268; Barton 1995). However, this decision is an indication that the UK courts will not allow this in the future. More importantly, the decision represents a shift of emphasis in policy from excessive cautiousness to judicial expediency. In *Genentech* and *Biogen* the Court of Appeal grappled with what one might term the "threshold" policy: should patent law be extended to this new technology? Here the issue is whether there is something inherently unpatentable about such inventions or which conflicts directly with other public policy considerations.

The clear message from the House of Lords in *Biogen* is that no such grounds exist for denying patents in principle. The policy which preoccupied the House of Lords is, however, what one might call the "operational" policy: what sort of monopolies should be granted? In balance here are considerations of fairness and reasonableness - one must offer patent protection as an incentive to innovate, while at the same time being careful not to close off the market to all but a few innovators. In this respect the decision in *Biogen* is encouraging as an indication that our courts are no longer dazzled by the complexities of the science and are willing to treat biotechnology as much as possible as any other field subject to the normal vagaries of the patent system. Unfortunately not all matters are settled by this decision.

Biogen before the European Patent Office

The European Patent Office also had occasion to examine the patentability of Biogen's invention, given that the patent in suit was a 'European' patent (*BIOGEN/Hepatitis B* [1995] EPOR 1). In the EPO the patent was granted for 11 Contracting States (Austria with less claims) and upheld by the Technical Board of Appeal. The invention was held to be non-obvious applying the test of "obvious to try with a reasonable expectation of success". The disparity with the UK in this respect has already been noted. That it should occur in the same case is entirely contrary to the spirit of harmonisation of the European patent system and augurs badly for future disputes over biotechnological inventions.

The EPO allowed priority to be claimed from Biogen 1 on the grounds that the prior document disclosed all of the "essential features" of the invention. These "must be either express, or be directly and unambiguously implied by the text. Missing elements which are to be recognised as essential only later on are thus not part of the disclosure." (See, for example, *COLLABORATIVE/Preprorennin* [1990] EPOR 361). The Board was unconcerned by the fact that some elements of the invention worked less successfully (the expression of surface antigen). The House of Lords was similarly unconcerned by this, but that is because it revoked that patent for excess of breadth and not for lack of efficacy. Unfortunately, the EPO was not concerned with the question of breadth. The conclusion which Lord Hoffmann drew from this was that his decision was not at odds with the EPO decision, because on other EPO jurisprudence his "breadth" conclusion is supported. He was at pains to stress that EPO decisions are highly persuasive in the UK as a matter of law, but nevertheless came to a diametrically opposed view on the validity of the patent. Undoubtedly, the House here acted as "a court of appeal from the EPO" (Karet 1997: 26) and gave rise to the anomaly of "selective validity" within the European patent system.

Finally, on the question of the degree of skill to be possessed by the notional expert in testing obviousness, the House of Lords in *Biogen* is silent, presumably leaving the authority of *Genentech* intact. This is to be compared with the approach of the EPO which has held that the biotech expert is a "cautious" individual, with a "conservative attitude" who would deem a transfer of technical knowledge to be obvious only if it involved "nothing out of the ordinary" (*GENENTECH/Expression in Yeast* [1996] EPOR 85 at 98).

Such disparities occur because no official hierarchy of fora exists in which to test consistently the validity of European patents. As the example of *Biogen* shows, this results in disharmony and disunity and can lead to a valid 'European' patent being declared invalid in national systems. If Europe is serious about having a truly harmonised patent system, this situation cannot be allowed to persist. The Community Patent Convention (CPC), which would introduce the first Europe-wide patent, contains provisions for a Community Common Appeal Court that would ensure consistency of approach. Unfortunately, it looks increasingly unlikely that the CPC will ever be brought into force. For the present, reform of the EPC can address the problems identified above.

What is needed is a single body, accepted as authoritative both by the EPO and national courts, which can deliver consistent and binding interpretations on European patent law. Two proposals for reform along such lines have recently been advanced. Sir Robin Jacob (1997) of the English High Court has suggested that the membership of the EPO's Enlarged Board of Appeal (EBA) comprise patent judges from national systems. This, he argues, would not only strengthen the position of the EBA within the European patent system, but would also help to ensure consistency towards the grant of patents in Europe. This is certainly true, and such a reform could be instituted with relative ease, but it maintains the division between the European patent system and the national patent systems, and relies on the goodwill of national judges to follow EBA decisions.

A more radical reform which would achieve all that Jacob proposes, and build a bridge between the two systems, has been proposed by Professor Jan Brinkof (1997). He advocates the establishment of a single European Patent Court, staffed by judges of the supreme courts of Contracting States, as a final forum of appeal to rule on matters of interpretation of patent law. In this way, a dispute such as *Biogen* would not leave all power in the hands of the appeal courts in national systems. Such a reform does, however, involve quite radical changes to the EPC, since it blurs the distinction between patent grant and patent enforcement, the latter being the exclusive domain of national systems at the present time. Also, decisions of such a European Patent Court would be binding on national courts, which is again a departure from the current practice of treating EPO decisions merely as "highly persuasive". Nevertheless, in the interests of maintaining the competitive edge of Europe in the global marketplace and ensuring that it continues to attract hi-tech industries such as biotechnology, reforms of this kind may be precisely what are required.

Morality

So far we have considered policy matters which reflect the economic concerns surrounding biotechnology and its promotion in the UK and Europe. A very important additional policy consideration in this field is that of morality. This has become a central issue in the grant of patents in Europe and has widened considerably the gap between Europe and the US in terms of the security offered to inventors and investors in the biotech field.

In *Diamond v Chakrabarty* 447 US 303, 66 L Ed 2d 144 (1980) the US Supreme Court refused to consider the morality of granting a patent over a genetically engineered oil-eating bacterium. It went as far as to state that, "Congress intended statutory subject matter to include anything under the sun that is made by man" (at 150). The court declared itself competent to rule only on the question of the economic value of granting a patent. Other values, such as the value of "life", the value of morally acceptable inventions and the value of a safe environment were deemed to be matters of "high policy" exclusively for Congress.

In stark contrast, Article 53 of the European Patent Convention provides:

> European patents shall not be granted in respect of -
>
> (a) inventions the publication or exploitation of which would be contrary to "ordre public" or morality, provided that the exploitation shall not be deemed to be so contrary merely because it is prohibited by law or regulation in some or all of the Contracting States;
>
> (b) plant or animal varieties or essentially biological processes for the production of plants or animals; this provision does not apply to microbiological processes or the products thereof.

In *HARVARD/ONCOmouse* [1990] EPOR 4 the claimed invention was to a genetically engineered mouse into which had been inserted a human cancer gene. In the USA a patent was granted in 1988, but in Europe the Examining Division of the EPO was faced with the argument that ONCOmouse failed the test under Article 53 both as an invention contrary to *ordre public*, and as an animal variety. Initially, the Examining Division declined to rule on the question of morality (much as the US Supreme Court had done in *Diamond*), but the Board of Appeal held that it must do so as a matter of law ([1990 EPOR 501). Following the advice of the Board, the Examining Division then held that the patent should be granted on the following grounds ([1991] EPOR 525).

First, the patent did *not* claim an animal variety because the specific wording of the application related to "non-human mammals". This was held to be much wider than mere "animal varieties" and therefore was not expressly excluded by Article 53(b).

Second, the question of the immorality of the invention was to be tested by balancing, on the one hand, the suffering of the animals and potential risks to the environment, and on the other, the potential benefits to humanity from the exploitation of such inventions. The Division accepted without question that the invention at issue was useful to humanity and that suffering to the animals was acceptable in the pursuit of cancer research.

Opposition proceedings were immediately instituted by 16 different groups and these proceedings remain undecided seven years on, so what little comfort was offered to the biotechnology industry from this case has long since dissipated. The ruling has, however, been attacked not just by those who would oppose grant but also by those who would favour patenting animals and other life forms. Arguments range from those which question the ability of patent examiners to rule on matters moral, to those which doubt the acceptability of the tests laid down in the decision, to those which question the appropriateness of including morality provisions in patent law at all.

Morality is certainly a highly subjective matter, and there is undeniable strength in the argument that patent examiners alone are not in a position to rule on such issues. Shortly after *ONCOmouse* in *Upjohn's Application* the morality test was used to deny a patent claim for a hairless oncomouse bred for research into human hair loss. Applying the balancing test, the EPO considered that the benefit to humanity did not outweigh the suffering to the animal and refused the patent (Nott, 1993: 47). Upjohn were able to redraft their application, however, by removing reference to the oncogene as a marker. The remaining claims were held to be valid and the patent allowed (Nott, 1995: 566).

We can see from this that the ONCOmouse "balance" test is utterly ill-equipped to control "immoral" inventions. That it can be drafted around hows a serious limitation on the role of patent examiners who can merely interpret the words in the patent claims. Furthermore, even when the test is applied with effect, it operates as an additional "utility" requirement, rather than a test of morality as such. Provided that enough benefit can be gained, it would appear that nothing can be *malum in se*.

Before examining any further EPO decisions, it must be appreciated that the policies underlying Article 53 are of two different kinds, only one of which concerns morality. Certainly, morality underpins subsection (a), although the Guidelines of the EPO (Section C-IV, 3.1.) have always envisaged an invention which the public would consider to be "so abhorrent that the grant of patent rights would be inconceivable". The exclusion of animal varieties in subsection (b) is also a concern about morality; it stems from the fact that prior to the EPC most national systems disallowed the patenting of animal life. However, the exclusion of plant varieties is not based on moral concerns, but rather concerns of double protection. In 1961 the Convention for the Protection of New Varieties of Plants (UPOV) was passed which established a *sui generis* plant protection right. Signatories to UPOV 1961 agreed to prohibit double protection under the Convention and patent law, and the reference to "plant varieties" in Article 53(b) of the EPC can be seen as an attempt to embody this in European patent law. In 1991 the UPOV Convention was revised, however, to allow joint protection for plants both by patents and plant variety right (PVR).

We can see, then, that the inclusion of plant and animal varieties within the same provision of the EPC should not be taken to mean that concerns about their patentability relate solely to issues of morality. That said, in *PLANT GENETIC SYSTEMS/Glutamine Synthesase Inhibitors* [1995] EPOR 357 the Technical Board of Appeal confirmed that moral concerns surrounding the exploitation of herbicide-resistant genetically engineered plants and their potential impact on the environment could be considered under Article 53(a). However, following *ONCOmouse*, the Board took a narrow view of morality and held that to deny the patent it would have to be proved that there was a likelihood of "serious prejudice" to the environment or that the invention was contrary to the conventionally accepted standards of conduct of European culture. It rejected survey and opinion poll evidence on the "immorality" of patenting as inconclusive and pointed out that genetic manipulation of plant life (and indeed animal life) has always been a part of European culture. Inventions which have this as their end cannot, therefore, be unpatentable *in se*. Furthermore, because no direct evidence could be produced that the invention in question would prejudice the environment the objections under 53(a) were disallowed. The Board refused even to consider a 'balance' of interests, as had happened in *ONCOmouse*, because "no sufficient evidence of actual disadvantages had been adduced" (at 373).

This is to interpret the morality provision very narrowly indeed. Evidence was led that potential risks from herbicide-resistant plants generally could be high, but no actual evidence regarding the claimed invention could be brought. Fortunately, this was so, but the attitude of the Board was that only if faced with hard evidence of actual risk having occurred to the environment from the invention would a patent be denied. Surely, however, if an invention has been allowed to pose a risk to the environment, it must have been placed in that environment. If this is so, the invention would be in the public domain; for the prospective patentee this is a problem because ultimately a patent would be refused for lack of novelty and/or obviousness. No prospective patentee will do such a thing, and therefore arguably prior to application there will never be any evidence of an actual risk to the environment. Those who are likely to oppose such patents will not be aware of the invention prior to publication of the patent and even once they become aware they will be unlikely to be able to adduce sufficient evidence of actual risk in the time between publication and grant. After grant, only nine months are available in which to object, which again is insufficient time to gather evidence of this kind. Thus, it would seem that the interpretation given to the morality provision in this case effectively renders it useless as a ground for refusal or revocation. It has been interpreted out of existence.

It should be noted, however, that the claims in the patent to the plant itself were nevertheless revoked under Article 53(b). It was held that because the genetically altered plant could reproduce and pass on its resistance in a relatively stable manner, it qualified as a "plant variety" and as such should be excluded from patentability. The argument that the plant was a product produced by a microbiological process was rejected because the insertion of the resistant gene was but one small part of the general process of replicating the plant. This stands in stark contrast to the *ONCOmouse* decision. There it was held that not only could the animals be claimed because they were not animal varieties, but also that the offspring of such animals could be claimed. In essence the animals were products-by-process, that is, they were the products of microbiological process; namely, genetic engineering techniques. This was so even although the mice would reproduce normally.

The Enlarged Board of Appeal refused to hold that these two decisions were in any way inconsistent (*Inadmissible referral* [1996] EPOR 505). It did so on the simple basis that what had been produced by PGS was a "plant variety" *as defined by* UPOV 1991. This is problematic for many reasons.

First, there is no basis in patent law for ruling that the definition of "plant varieties" under Article 53(b) need have anything to do with UPOV. Indeed, why should it, given that the 1991 provisions could not have been contemplated when the EPC was drafted.

Second, the definition of plant varieties in UPOV 1991 is more generous to plant breeders than UPOV 1961, which means paradoxically that it will exclude more from patent protection, and in particularly probably all forms of genetically engineered plants.

Third, there must be serious doubt as to whether one can persist in excluding plant varieties from patent protection given that the original reason for the exclusion has been removed by the 1991 Convention.

Finally, it is hard to see how one can in all conscience reconcile *Plant Genetic Systems* with *ONCOmouse* when at one level of abstraction that which has been done in each case is essentially the same, yet different outcomes are reached. Moreover, neither exclusion has remained true to the original policy underlying its existence. "Animals" but not "animal varieties" are patentable (morally, rather difficult to justify), and "plant varieties" are excluded from patent protection by reference to a convention which now permits their patentability.

The final "moral maze" to be negotiated is that concerning human genetic material. In *HOWARD FLOREY/Relaxin* [1995] EPOR 541 the patent in suit concerned H2-relaxin, a protein produced by pregnant women to ease childbirth. Before the Opposition Division it was argued that the granting of the patent was tantamount to slavery of women because it involved the dismemberment of women and the sale of those parts, that it was offensive to human dignity because it involved the use of pregnant women for profit, and finally that because DNA was "life" itself, patenting of human DNA was intrinsically immoral. As in previous cases it was held that "morality" should be interpreted narrowly, and the submissions of the opponents were rejected.

Concerning the use of tissue taken from pregnant women, the Division relied exclusively on the importance of individual consent: if the women from whom the original material was taken consented, then what is done with the tissue cannot be immoral. The Division considered the multiple uses to which human tissue is already put without impinging on human dignity, and that no other women need donate tissue for the invention to be repeated because new material could easily be produced using genetic engineering techniques.

The Division also rejected out of turn the arguments that DNA was "life". DNA, it said, is not life, but a chemical substance that carries information. Indeed, even if it were life, to grant a patent over such samples is not to give an exclusive property right in the persons from whom the tissue was taken: "no woman is affected in any way by the present patent" (at 550 -1).

This decision represents a clear policy decision by the EPO to favour the work of the biotechnology industry over the concerns of many that the work is somehow morally corrupt or corrupting from the perspective of human dignity. The individualistic approach of the Division to the question of consent, however, ignores the fact that the human genome is in very large part common to all of humanity, and masks wider concerns that many sectors of society have about its exploitation.

The EPO has chosen to treat human material in the same way as animal and plant material in an attempt to offer some consistency of approach for the biotechnology industry. Morally, however, we do treat humans differently from animals and plants, and we find many ways to justify this. Arguably, then, it should be more difficult to manipulate and exploit human genetic material free of moral constraint. The approach of the EPO to the question of morality does not seem to allow for such subtlety of approach. The crude utilitarian calculus which is adopted leaves no scope for deontologically-grounded arguments that some things are wrong in themselves and that from time to time a moral stance must be taken. That said, the practice in the USA has been to allow the patenting of human gene sequences and other materials provided that they have a known function. A similar view has recently been expounded by the European Commission's Group of Advisers on the Ethical Implications of Biotechnology (1996).

In June 1997 the US National Bioethics Advisory Commission reported to President Clinton that a ban should be imposed on the cloning of humans in light of the work carried out by the Roslin Institute in Edinburgh. This, however, did not rule out cloning research on embryos as such, only the implantation of cloned embryos *in utero* (Wilson 1997). Such a rare move to curtail the work of the biotechnology industry is informative, not so much for the insight that it offers into the US moral position, but more for the extreme caution with which disapproval is expressed. Even although the work in question involves human material, regulation is kept to a minimum to protect as much as possible the on-going work of the industry.

Understandably, the EPO has come under significant pressure to adopt a similar approach in the economic interests of Europe. The tension between economics and morality is palpable and explains in very large part the unacceptable situation which currently persists. For all interest groups this is unsatisfactory.

The EC Draft Directive

Recognising the need for reform the European Commission produced in 1988 a Draft Directive on the Legal Protection of Biotechnological Inventions, designed to clarify matters and redress imbalances (COM (88) 496 final - SYN 159). The depth of concern about the work of the biotechnology industry was forcibly expressed, however, in March 1995 when the Draft was defeated by the European Parliament exercising for the first time its right of veto under the Maastricht Treaty (OJ C68, 20 March 1995, p 26, COM (92) 589 final - SYN 159). A new draft currently awaits adoption (COM (95) 661 final of 13 December 1995). It is far from clear, however, that it will do anything of substance to alleviate the crisis in Europe over biotechnology.

The following points show the inadequacies of the Draft Directive and indicate that it should once again be rejected.

First, the text concerns solely the laws in Member States and does nothing to ensure consistency of approach toward the interpretation of European patent law. Thus, the problems outlined above concerning the need for a harmonised approach to the law and a "bridge" between the EPO and national systems will remain.

Second, although the current draft is more explicit that parts of the human body *are* patentable provided that they are no longer in their natural state, this does not address the concerns of those who object to the permissibility of patenting human body parts at all. It was essentially on this ground that the original version fell, and the new wording will do nothing to satisfy those who objected then and who continue to object today.

Third, the draft retains the distinction between the patentability of animals/plants and animal and plant varieties, the distinction between biological processes and micro-biological processes and the morality test laid down by the EPO in *ONCOMouse*. However, no further guidance is offered on how these provisions are to be applied. Given that these are to be interpreted by the EPO, it is difficult to see how the approach currently adopted by that body will be any different even if the Directive were adopted.

The Preamble to the Draft recognises the strong economic reasons why disharmony in Europe cannot be allowed to persist. Differences of approach between Member States and between Europe and other countries act as barriers to trade and are a disincentive to investors. It is hard to see how adoption of the Draft Directive would ameliorate this. The proposal is very much one based on compromise, yet what has not been undertaken is a sufficient review of the policies which underlie patent law.

A policy designed to advance economic interests must mean strong patent rights and parity of protection with other trading blocks. Unfortunately, this clashes head-on with morality issues, for a policy which enshrines moral concerns means taking a stance on patentability with clear consequences for Europe's economic future. The failure of the Draft Directive comes in trying to advance simultaneously both policies. But are these policies of equal validity? The best way to test this is to ask whether the underlying aims of each policy can be achieved by their incorporation into patent law.

The predominant aim of an economic policy is to encourage investment and innovation through strong protection. The entire history of the patent system stands as testament to the success of this policy in patent law. What, however, are the aims of a moral policy? These include prevention of offensive conduct, protection from harm, and encouragement of respect for human beings and other life-forms. In addition, a moral policy applied in a particular context must take its place in the wider community of moral values and should exist in harmony with such other values. Can such aims be achieved by the incorporation of moral policy in European patent law? It is submitted that they cannot, at least not to a degree which justifies an unsatisfactory compromise with economic policy such as we see in the Draft Directive.

The crucial determining factor in this debate is the question of what morality provisions in patent law can realistically achieve. If successful, the result is denial of patent grant. This registers a degree of disapproval about a particular "invention", and a direct consequence may be that others are dissuaded from inventing, if the "incentive theory" of patents is to be believed. But even if this is so, it is an extremely inefficient way of achieving that goal. Unfortunately no other means are available, for what morality provisions cannot do is prevent the creation of the invention itself. In other words, the refusal of a patent cannot prevent "immoral conduct" taking place. This has direct and serious implications for the other aims of a moral policy. If creation itself cannot be prevented, then the harm with which one is concerned similarly cannot be controlled. ONCOmouse will still suffer and the moral standards of our society will still be compromised by the use of human material in therapeutics. Arguably, to object to an "immoral" invention at the stage of patent grant will always be to lock the cage door after the mouse has scurried off. If one is concerned with suffering to animals, then that concern should surely be directed at the act of creation itself, and not at the act of protection.

Two standard "moral" objections are often advanced. First, that it is commercialisation which is objectionable, particularly in the context of human material. Second, it is the exploitative nature of what is done that is offensive. The common response is that we do these things already in other contexts. Whereas this is true, it is a weak argument to plead that two wrongs make a right. Nonetheless, consistency of moral approach must also be part of a moral policy, and one cannot ignore the fact that *what* biotechnology does is no different to what we have always done; namely, manipulate our environment. Furthermore, the reasons *why* we use biotechnology to do this are the same reasons we have always advanced: perceived benefit to our species. Indeed, arguably all that is different about biotechnology is *how* and *how well* we mould other life forms to our own ends. This must lead us to ask whether what is done is indeed a "wrong". At best the argument can stand only in relation to human material.

To argue that the grant of a patent in necessarily exploitative is to misunderstand the nature of patents. A patent is simply a negative right to exclude others; it is not a licence to exploit free from further constraint. All inventions - patented or unpatented - are subject to national laws regulating practices in line with commonly accepted social standards, and all "morally sensitive" practices such as the production of genetically modified organisms are subject to regulation. (See, for example, Council Directive on the contained use of genetically modified micro-organisms 90/219/EEC, 1990 OJ L117/1; Council Directive on the deliberate release into the environment of genetically modified organisms 90/220/EEC, 1990 OJ L117/15). This is not to suggest that this in any way desensitised these practices from a moral perspective; rather it is to propose that regulatory laws and bodies are a more suitable focus for those who take moral issue with biotechnology.

Moral objections to patenting at best permit a stance to be taken - but even if the battle is won the victory is entirely pyrrhic. Such objections are misplaced in terms of time, forum, means and end. They come at the wrong time to prevent creation and are addressed to a forum which is powerless to do anything other than grant or deny a negative legal right of exclusion. Thus, even if the means used are successful, the end which one seeks cannot be achieved beyond registering a degree of moral distaste and encouraging inventors to go where protection *is* available.

One need only take a small step back from the debate to see that at the heart of the "morality" objections to biotechnology patents are concerns about the work of the biotechnology industry itself. This is turn calls into question the role of the law in regulating that work. Thus, arguably, the debate is really one of deciding if the law of patents is the best, or even a good way of regulating the biotechnology industry. It is not, and a failure to recognise this will only perpetuate the problems currently beleaguering Europe.

Conclusion

What then should be done for patent law? If it is accepted that the dominant policy in this field should be that of encouraging economic development, then current inconsistencies could be remedied by a three-fold process of reform of the EPC itself. First, an ultimate court of appeal for the European patent system could be established along the lines suggested above. Second, the distinction in Article 53(b) between animals and plants and varieties of such should be removed since on neither policy ground is the distinction sustainable. Third, Article 53(a) should similarly be repealed. Alternatively, if it is thought desirable to retain some reference to *ordre public*, then an express provision should be included making clear the precise (narrow) terms within which it will operate.

The depth of concern about the lack of harmony in European patent law is evident in the Commissions's *Green Paper on the Community Patent System in*

Europe: Promoting Innovation Through Patents (COM 97 314 final; 24 June 1997) which seeks views on possible reforms to extricate Europe from the current stalemate surrounding the Community Patent Convention. Although the paper does not deal with all of the concerns expressed in this work, it does propose reform of the European patent hierarchy, including the introduction of exclusive powers of grant and revocation for the EPO and appeals to the European Court of First Instance and the Court of Justice. Such opportunities must be seized to ensure that Europe assumes its rightful place in the next century as a worthy competitor for the United States and Japan in the field of biotechnology and, indeed, all other new and emerging technologies.

Bibliography

Barton, J. H., (1995). Patent scope in biotechnology. *International Review of Industrial Property and Copyright Law*, **26**, 605.

Brinkof, J. J., (1997). The desirability, necessity and feasibility of co-operation between courts in the fields of European patent law. *European Intellectual Property Review*, **5**, 226.

Crespi, S., (1995). Biotechnology, broad claims and the EPC. *European Intellectual Property Review*, **6**, 267.

Ernst & Young, (1997). *Biobusiness*. Ernst & Young.

Group of Advisers on the Ethical Implications of Biotechnology to the European Commission, (1996). Luxembourg, Official Publications of the European Communities.

Jacob, R., (1997). The enlarged Board of Appeal of the EPO: a proposal. *European Intellectual Property Review*, **5**, 224.

Karet, I., (1997). Delivering the goods? The House of Lords' decision in *Biogen v Medeva*. *European Intellectual Property Review*, **1**, 21.

Nott, R., (1993). Plants and animals: why they should be protected by patent and variety rights. *Patent World*, July/August, 45.

Nott, R., (1995). The biotech directive: does Europe need a new draft? *European Intellectual Property Review*, **12**, 563.

Wilmut, I., Schnieke, A. E., McWhir, J., Kind, A. J., and Campbell, K. H. S., (1997). Viable offspring from fetal and adult mammalian cells. *Nature*, **385**, 810, February 27.

Wilson, P., (1997). US ethics panel urges ban on human cloning. Reuters, 8 June 1997.

Intellectual Property and the Internet

Charlotte Waelde

Synopsis

Mention the Internet to some, and their eyes will instantly glaze over; the Internet is something applicable only to computer nerds and poor lost souls wandering in cyberspace. This attitude is less prevalent than it used to be as the possibilities of the Internet for world-wide communication, information dissemination and commercial opportunity become more apparent. The communication of information lies at the heart of the Internet, whether by way of text, sound or pictures. It is now generally accepted that "terrestrial" laws, in particular intellectual property laws, apply with equal force to the information whizzing around in cyberspace. With the increase of commercial interest in the Internet, these laws are being applied to disputes arising in very novel situations, and there is a considerable struggle to make the law fit the facts. This article examines three areas where this stress is particularly apparent: the temporary reproduction right in copyright; the legality of hypertext links; and the interaction between trade marks and domain names. In each case, the terrestrial laws were drafted at a time when the concept of the Internet was little more than a gleam in the eye of an academic. The laws are now being used by commercial factions who have their own commercial goals to pursue, with results shaping the Internet for all users, and alteration of the carefully moderated checks and balances underpinning these laws. This article examines these shifts, and questions whether the use of these laws is the best way forward for the orderly development of the Internet, or whether we have arrived at such a stage where a "law of cyberspace" should be developed.

* * * * *

The impact of digitisation and the growth of the Internet hold immense opportunities for the exchange of information around the world on a scale never before possible. Communication of information is possible on a "one to one" basis, by way of email; on a "one to many" basis, through moderated and other discussion groups; and on a "one to all" basis, by creating a website, or joining a public discussion group. The content can be as diverse and varied as traditional forms of communication; it can be personal, educational, for information or commercial. The means by which the information is transmitted can be almost as varied as traditional forms of media, by text, by pictures and by sound. It can be created and disseminated by a single person or organisation with Internet access. Lately the commercial sector has been particularly enamoured of this form of communication, and the potential it offers them to reach an audience around the world at little cost, at least by comparison with using traditional media to distribute news of their wares. These commercial developments have led some to dub the Internet "the world-wide market place".

However, these developments are posing both perceived and actual dangers to owners of *inter alia* intellectual property rights. The information which is transmitted and exchanged all over the world can be modified, copied and further disseminated very easily and at little cost. Traditional concepts of the ways in which intellectual property rights in this information are created and infringed are under attack. Also being challenged are the underlying reasons for the existence of those rights in the first place. Intellectual property protection has historically grown by way of a balance and counter balance between competing interests; between monopoly and free competition; between the rights of creators to benefit from their work, and the interests of users to have free access to information. These traditional balances are being re-examined and re-evaluated in the light of the latest technological developments.

These tensions are illustrated in a number of scenarios being played out by the different factions who have an interest in the Internet. The extent of the right of reproduction, protected by the law of copyright, as it applies to surfing the Internet is under scrutiny, and pitching commercial interests against other users; commercial concerns would like to control all reproductions; other users, on the other hand, argue that a degree of "free use" of information is essential if the Internet is to flourish. Commercial interests are also at the forefront in the dispute over linking web pages by way of hypertext links. Again, existing intellectual property laws, and in particular copyright, are being used to challenge this behaviour. The result is that the whole basis on which the Internet is constructed, that of a seamless web of links, is in danger of being undermined, to the detriment of all users. Commercial bodies are also using existing laws to further their own aims; pitching one commercial interest against another. This is illustrated in the way that existing intellectual property laws are being used in the trade mark/domain name dispute; traditional concepts of trade mark infringement are being stretched in the arena of cyberspace to further commercial aims.

A further problem for the development of the Internet is burgeoning regulation. National, regional and international bodies are all vying to have some say in how the Internet should be run and regulated. National regulatory bodies are concerned because the Internet has an effect on their nationals; information that national regulatory bodies might wish to censor if it was distributed in newspapers or broadcast, is suddenly readily available on the Internet; thus these authorities want to regulate the Internet in accordance with their own recognised culture and standards. International bodies, who recognise that territorial solutions are not necessarily the most suitable for the Internet are attempting to develop international solutions that would be applicable to all, but in so doing, are threatening to overwhelm users under the weight of compliance costs. The danger is that the philosophy underpinning the development of the Internet, that of freedom of speech and interaction and the ability to transmit information freely and quickly from one source to another, is being undermined. When national authorities clamp down on Internet activities in accordance with their own terrestrial laws, this has a world-wide effect. A good example is the reaction of the Bavarian authorities when it became apparent in 1995 that newsgroups containing obscene and pornographic material were available to CompuServe subscribers in Germany. They ordered CompuServe to terminate those links. The practical effect is that all subscribers to CompuServe are subject to German laws on pornography and obscenity. The same would apply to any form of censorship that any national authority chose to apply to the Internet. Another example may be provided by the recent arrest of a CompuServe manager in Germany for "knowingly allowing images of child pornography, violent sex, and sex with animals from news groups from the Internet to be made accessible to customers of CompuServe Germany" (*Financial Times*, 13 May 1997).

This article will analyse the discussion and the disputes in three main areas:

- the temporary reproduction right in copyright,
- the legality of hypertext links
- the interaction between trade marks and domain names.

Each of these areas illustrates the shifting balances in intellectual property law, the ways in which commercial interests are shaping the Internet, and attempts by regulatory authorities to create some sort of order in the threatened disorder.

Copyright and the Internet: the temporary right of reproduction.

The extent of the right to control reproduction, the most fundamental right attaching to a work protected by copyright, is currently one focus of discussion in the context of the Internet. Few commentators dispute that the law of copyright is applicable to Internet activities; the question now is whether the current law of copyright is sufficient or too all-embracing for the new scenarios that are encountered with the technology. One of the traditional reasons given for protecting a work by copyright is that by allowing the author or owner to control the reproduction of her work, she can thereby receive a reward, usually in the form of financial gain. This in turn encourages her to create yet more works. Another view is that an author has the moral right to exploit her work. However, whatever the justification, the right has never been one of absolute monopoly, and is balanced in favour of users in a number of ways:

- by the requirement that a work is original before it is protected by copyright;
- by the requirement that a work be copied before there is infringement;

- through involuntary licensing schemes;
- through notions of "fair dealing or fair use";
- through the limit on the time for which a work is protected by copyright

Traditionally works protected by copyright have been disseminated by way of hard copies - on paper, films, photographs, and, more recently, on CD Rom. One of the underlying characteristics is that, barring physical destruction, the original work and any copies are permanent. But the Internet has now transformed the position. It is perfectly possible to create a transient copy of a work, by pulling that work on to a computer screen. That work is not then stored, but once the computer is turned off, the copy disappears. A fierce debate now rages around the extent to which the reproduction right belonging to the author or owner should extend to this transient or temporary copy. In this discussion, there is a perceptible shift in the balance between the interests of creators and users; the approach appears to be on how the economic interests of the creators can be satisfied as the primary concern, rather than on how a balance can be attained.

There are those who argue that to protect commercial interests, every reproduction of a work over the Internet without authorisation, however transient, should amount to an infringement of the copyright in that work. Thus, surfing the Internet and calling images onto the screen of a computer would amount to an infringement. Such protection would allow right-holders to control their work, to grant licences or assignations and thus to make a return from their investment. However, with the new technology used by the Internet, such a far-reaching right could have some unexpected consequences. Indeed, if it were taken to its logical conclusion in the "non-Internet" world, an image of a work protected by copyright reproduced in a mirror would infringe copyright! The way in which the Internet is constructed means that material protected by copyright is passed from one computer to another, and along the way is stored and copied by many different host computers provided by those supplying the equipment making up the backbone of the network. The sheer volume of information that circulates through the Internet means that the providers of this equipment have little idea of the content of the information being copied and disseminated through their facilities,[1] and little chance to find out. Making such providers liable for copying information would undoubtedly mean that the development of the Internet would be hampered: they would not wish to be liable for actions for copyright infringement, and would therefore be unwilling to provide the infrastructure needed.

The solution apparently emerging from the discussion is that a transient copy should be covered by a right of reproduction where it has an economic effect for the right-holder. In other words, if the reproduction could have been exploited by the right-holder for economic gain, then she should have the right to control the reproduction. An example would be where a copy of a word processing program was held on a server within a local area network (LAN) rather than individual copies being loaded on to personal computers (PCs). Each time the software was used by the PC, or called up from the server on the LAN, there would in effect only be a transient copy. Nevertheless, making such a copy would have an economic effect for the right-holder who would licence only one copy of the software rather than a copy for each PC.

This approach shows the beginnings of a two-tier system that could be taken as the basis for a transient reproduction right on the Internet. On the one hand, a liberal "hands off" attitude to those who have placed information voluntarily on the Internet, such as marketing and advertising information which is not, and is not intended, to be re-distributed for economic gain. By contrast, transient reproductions of software and the acquisition of information from commercial databases, such as articles and case reports which would otherwise be distributed by way of hard copy or over the Internet with a charge, should all be covered by the transient reproduction right. Current difficulties arise not only because there is no international consensus on whether this transient reproduction right should exist, but also because some countries legislating for this right do not distinguish clearly between the circumstances when it may apply. Rather, the transient reproduction right tends to be a blanket right in favour of the right-holder, subject only perhaps to the "fair use" provisions applicable to other forms of reproduction. The consequence is that some sort of implied consent to copy, granted by the right-holder, has to be found in cases of "innocent infringement".

In the UK, a reproduction which will infringe copyright includes reproducing a work in any material form, and also storing a work by electronic means. Copying includes the making of copies which are transient or incidental to some other use of the work. This is generally taken to mean that merely surfing the Internet - pulling images from the web and simply looking at them on a PC - is an infringement of copyright if effected without authorisation.

However, as hinted above, a full transient reproduction right is by no means universally accepted, because it is seen by some as upsetting the balance between users and creators. Indeed, one of the most hotly contested areas at the 1996 Diplomatic Conference held in Geneva under the auspices of the World Intellectual Property Organisation (WIPO) was the extent to which a temporary right of reproduction should or should not be included in the new Copyright Treaty which was finally adopted at Geneva in December of that year. The initial proposal for the Treaty contained an Article which provided that the reproduction of works, whether permanent or temporary, was a right exclusive to the author. Exceptions to the right would have allowed signatory states to legislate within the confines of Article 9(2) of the Berne Convention to make exceptions to this exclusive right provided they did not prejudice the legitimate expectations of the author. The effect would have been to grant the right to the authors, with only limited exceptions for users. It was argued by some that the proposal contained an entirely novel rule, and by others that it merely represented existing law.

One of the fundamental objections to the inclusion of this article related to public access to information over the Internet (see further Goldberg 1997). As with the temporary reproduction right granted in the UK, every act of surfing the net, and pulling information on to a screen would have been an infringement; a result considered too draconian and far-reaching by many delegates. Another objection was that the proposed wording of the Article would not have allowed exceptions to be provided for infrastructure and other service providers; transient copies of packets of information passed around the network, copied by and held on servers and host computers, would have constituted infringement. This was unacceptable to many countries, and ultimately no agreement was attained on the temporary reproduction right. An Agreed Statement was prepared confirming that the reproduction right provided for in the Treaty did not address the temporary copying question. Development of this point is therefore currently with national legislatures and courts within the confines of their international and regional obligations.

The question of the transient reproduction right has also been taxing the European Commission. As part of proposals to harmonise the law in relation to intellectual property rights, the Commission has produced a follow-up paper (COM (96) 568 final, 20.11.96) to its Green Paper on Copyright and Related Rights (COM (95) 382 final 19.7.1995), proposing four areas for further harmonisation. These include the reproduction right, a right of communication to the public, provision of remedies against the circumvention or abuse of electronic management systems and the distribution right. The follow-up paper recognises that whereas all Member States provide for an exclusive reproduction right for all categories of right-holders, the scope of the right and exemptions from it differ, particularly in relation to transient acts of reproduction. The intention behind the follow up paper is clear: the transient right of reproduction will be covered by the reproduction right, but will then be cut down by means of a legal licence either with or without remuneration. However, the specific areas which will be the subject of the licence have yet to be decided.

As can be seen, responses to the issues posed by the temporary reproduction right are currently piecemeal, with no international consensus about how, or indeed whether, to legislate for the right. Even for those countries which incorporate the right in domestic legislation, it is argued that to make someone liable for copyright infringement each time she surfs the net and calls an image on to a computer screen is unrealistic. Much of the time, information is put on to the Internet voluntarily; to say that the surfer then infringes copyright makes a mockery of a law which is honoured more in the breach than otherwise.

Copyright licences

One way in which the all embracing nature of the right can be mitigated is by the concept of the implied copyright licence. But what sort of balance could be achieved by using these licences in relation to the Internet? Could they balance the interests of creators and users? Or would they favour one interest group over another?

Implied copyright licences may be available in the UK where the copyright owner intended that a work protected by copyright should be copied and disseminated. For example, where an author sends a letter to an editor of a newspaper, a licence will be implied that the editor may reproduce that letter in the newspaper (*Springfield v Thame* (1903) 89 LT 242). Applying this by analogy to the temporary reproduction right, where a work is voluntarily placed on the Internet, a licence can be implied that the information will be read, and thus copied albeit temporarily by the browser. But how far does, or should, this licence extend?

An interesting recent case on implied copyright licences in the context of distribution of computer software and the Internet was heard in the Australian Federal Court, *Trumpet Software Pty Ltd v OzEmail Pty Ltd* [1996] 18 (12) EIPR 69. The reasoning in this case could have wider implications for dissemination of information protected by copyright over the Internet.

Trumpet marketed software as "shareware". OzEmail approached Trumpet with a view to incorporating this software with their own, and selling it on a commercial basis. Trumpet refused consent. Despite this OzEmail made changes to the software, bundled it with some of their own and distributed it over the Internet. Trumpet contended that this infringed their copyright in their software. OzEmail argued that because the software had been distributed as shareware, it included an implied licence that it could be distributed and reproduced by those who so wished. The court held that, in the absence of express restrictions, two particular conditions would be implied into the licence: firstly, that the software was to be distributed without modification, addition or deletion; and secondly, that the software should be distributed in its entirety. By analogy with this reasoning, where a work protected by copyright is placed on the Internet (with no express restrictions as to use) then a licence can be implied to permit the distribution and reproduction of the work without modification.

But does this go far enough? Trumpet also contended that the software should be distributed without charge or other commercial gain. This term was rejected by the court. However, if such a condition was implied, this would mark an important right for the author, and indeed for general dissemination of information around the Internet. Take the example of an article voluntarily (i.e. not for a charge) placed on the Internet. Simply reading that article on-line would not constitute an infringement. If, however, a third party wanted to make a commercial gain from that information, for example by incorporating it into a fee-paying site, or by selling hard copies, that would have an economic impact on the right-holder and thus constitute infringement.[2]

As with the transient reproduction right, this analysis moves the focus from a balance between the rights of the creators and users to the economic right of the creator as the primary basis for protection, certainly in those jurisdictions where the main purpose of protection lies with the moral right of the author. At the same time it reflects the implications of the changing technology and means by which information is disseminated. If followed elsewhere, the effect is likely to be more circumstances in which information can be distributed "for free", because in the majority of cases information is placed on the Internet voluntarily, with the intention that it should be reproduced on a PC by users surfing the Internet. This approach has the advantages of ensuring that the surfer does not infringe the law each time she surfs the net.

Copyright, trade marks and hypertext links

Hypertext links are a fundamental feature of the Internet, the one that makes it a seamless web of information. A hypertext link takes the surfer effortlessly from one source of information, located at one website, to another, simply by clicking on the relevant path. However, the legality of these hypertext links have been called into question both expressly and by implication by way of application of the law of copyright and trade marks; by the case of *The Shetland Times v Dr Jonathan Wills* 1997 SLT 669 in Scotland; by *Trumpet v OzEmail* (above) in Australia, and by *Ticketmaster v Microsoft* in the US (for which see *http://www.news.com/news/item/0,4,10157,00 html*).

These disputes are being fought between those who have commercial interests on the Internet, and are linked by a similar theme. A website usually consists of a home page which will carry general information about the website provider, and sometimes advertisements sponsored by third parties. This home page is then linked, by hypertext links, to further pages on the same website which carry more specific information such as news stories, information on products and so on. The concept is similar to a newspaper where the headlines are placed on the front page; the reader turns the pages to get detailed information. The website will also carry links to other websites. These links to other websites need not access the home page of the second web site, but rather may lead directly to pages deeper within the second site. In the same way, a second website may link to the first, but not through the home page, so again going deeper within the site. The effect is to by-pass the home page of the website to which a link is being made, thus skipping over the information on who is providing the site, and any other material contained on the home page, notably advertising. Some companies are taking exception to this type of activity, and are using existing intellectual property laws in an attempt to prohibit links which by-pass their home pages. However, in their zeal to protect their own commercial interests, companies are questioning the legality of linking. But without linking, the Internet will no longer have its present form of the seamless web.

In *The Shetland Times v Dr Jonathan Wills*, the *Shetland Time*s, a newspaper, established a website which contained some of the news items, pictures and stories which appeared in its hard copy editions. The home page carried not only the title of the newspaper and headlines, but also a number of advertisements. Access to the stories and pictures via the hypertext link was gained by clicking on the required headline. Dr Wills, trading as the *Shetland News*, also established a website on which appeared a heading "The Shetland News", a number of headlines repeated verbatim from the *Shetland Times* and a number of advertisements. Dr Wills set up his web site in such a way that by clicking on the relevant headline, the hypertext link would take the reader directly to the story and pictures prepared by the *Shetland Times* on the *Shetland Times* web pages. The result of this was to by-pass the front page of the *Shetland Times*.

The *Shetland Times* sought an interim interdict on the basis that the actions of the *Shetland News* amounted to an infringement of copyright on two grounds. The one relevant to this discussion is that the headlines originating with the *Shetland Times*, and repeated verbatim by the *Shetland News* constituted a cable programme within the meaning of section 7 of the Copyright Designs and Patents Act 1988 (CDPA),[3] and that the web page owned by the *Shetland News* was a cable programme service. Including the cable programme within the cable programme service amounted to an infringement of copyright within the meaning of section 20 CDPA. Lord Hamilton found that the pursuers had a *prima facie* case and granted interim interdict, prohibiting further use of the links until a full trial of the case.

The generally accepted view to date in the UK has been that the Internet is not a cable programme service within the definition in section 7 CDPA because it has an interactive nature, and such services are expressly excluded from the scope of the definition. However, by finding a *prima facie* case on these grounds, the legality of the inclusion of hypertext links within web pages is called into question, as each hypertext link involves the taking of some information from the second website and its inclusion within the first. If at the full hearing there is a finding for the *Shetland Times*, this will leave a question mark hanging over the legality of hypertext links on the Internet, certainly under Scots law. Reading between the lines, what really upset the *Shetland Times* was not the linking of the pages *per se*, but rather that the linking of the pages by-passed the *Shetland Times* home page, and therefore the advertising which appeared on that page. This would have made it difficult for the *Shetland Times* to attract advertising revenue. However, by using the existing law of copyright, drafted at a time at which the explosive development of the Internet was not foreseen, to pursue their own commercial goals, the future development of the Internet is being put at risk. The case is indicative of the consequences resulting from the application of current legislation to the Internet although it was not drafted with this technology in mind.

A question over the legality of hypertext links can also raised by drawing an analogy with *Trumpet v OzEmail*, where the Australian court found that the software should be distributed in its entirety, without modification. As mentioned already, a hypertext link often leads, not to the home page of the second website, but to some specific information that may be on offer within that particular site. In other words, the information contained on the second site is not distributed in its entirety, but rather specific parts are highlighted. If a copyright licence to reproduce the information can be implied because it has been placed on the Internet voluntarily, it may not extend far enough to cover linking to the second website. This is because the information which is reproduced from the second website is modified. The information called up from the second website would therefore constitute an infringement of copyright.

The third dispute to challenge the legality of hypertext links, but this time using trade mark law as the basis of the action, is *Ticketmaster v Microsoft*. Ticketmaster has filed a suit in the US alleging trade mark dilution by Microsoft. Ticketmaster sells *inter alia* tickets for Broadway shows, and has set up a web site to sell these tickets over the Internet. Microsoft, trading through Sidewalk, has linked to the Ticketmaster web site, not through the home page, but rather to deeper within the site. Ticketmaster alleges that Microsoft has

INTELLECTUAL PROPERTY AND THE INTERNET 73

therefore diluted the value of its trade marks. The case is yet to be heard, but if there is a finding in favour of Ticketmaster, it will give yet another weapon to these commercial entities using existing legislation to shape the Internet to meet their own interests. The ripples from this will affect all users.[4]

Existing intellectual property laws are being applied to Internet activities in a formalistic manner, with the result that while commercial entities are defending and getting answers in what they see to be their own (short term) interests, the results of their litigation could have a profound effect on the way in which the Internet develops, to the likely detriment of all users.

Trade marks and the Internet

The function of trade mark protection is quite different from that of copyright. Whereas copyright exists to allow authors to exploit the fruits of their labour, or a moral right to control that work, the rationale for trade marks lies in the consumer society. A trade mark serves as an indication of origin, allowing a trader a limited monopoly in the use of a mark when used in connection with goods and services. In common with the monopoly in relation to copyright - the balance between creators' rights to control reproduction and users to have free access to information - so there is a carefully balanced monopoly in relation to trade mark law; between the right of the trade mark owner to use a registered trade mark in respect of goods and services for which it is registered, and the right of competitors to use the same or a similar mark in relation to dissimilar goods and services so long as there is no public confusion. Trade mark law in no way gives the registered trade mark owner a monopoly in relation to the goods or services themselves. As with copyright, this careful balance is now being challenged.

The application of trade mark law to Internet activities has the same ingredients as the disputes discussed above in relation to copyright: the extent to which commercial interests are shaping, through litigation, the development of the Internet; and questions of regulation of the Internet when trade mark disputes arise. The response of those who see themselves charged with the responsibility of regulating the allocation of domain names, and the confusion that has resulted has only served to highlight the dangers of taking a piecemeal and at times blinkered approach to the international nature of the Internet.

Trade marks and domain names

Much litigation has surfaced recently in relation to domain names, and their interaction with trade marks.

A domain name is part of the address of a computer on the Internet. An example is "www.microsoft.com", where "Microsoft", the second-level domain name, is usually a description of the organisation which has registered the address, and is chosen because it is easily recognisable. ".com" is the top level domain name and denotes the type of entity which has registered the name. There are a number of generic top level domains, including ".com" used by commercial entities, and ".org" used by international organisations. These are registered in the United States and are viewed by those who use them as "international" domain names. There are also a number of country top-level domains: for example ".uk" for the United Kingdom, and ".de" for Germany.

Registered trade mark rights are granted by national authorities under domestic legislation that may be shaped by international obligations such as the obligations imposed on signatory states under the Paris Convention for the Protection of Industrial Property 1883, the Madrid Agreement concerning the International Registration of Marks 1891; the Protocol relating to the Madrid Agreement concerning the International Registration of Marks 1989, and the TRIPs Agreement 1994. A domain name is registered by one of the bodies set up around the world to administer the handling of these addresses, such as Network Solutions Inc (NSI) in the USA. The Internet Assigned Numbers Authority (IANA) acts under authority from the US Government and the Internet Society (ISOC) and is funded by the National Science Foundation (NSF). IANA allocates blocks of numeric IP addresses to NSI, which has overall authority for IP addresses, domain names and other Internet parameters. The function of allocating domain names in the US is in the hands of InterNic, an offshoot of NSI. In the UK, the body responsible for registering addresses under the .uk top level domain is Nominet. The difficulty over the interaction between trade mark law and domain names in the context of the Internet is that one domain name is for world-wide use, and no two domain names can be identical. There may be a number of people or entities who consider themselves to be "entitled" in a loose sense of the term to a particular domain name. Take the example of the name "Fellowes". In the UK, "Fellowes" may be the registered trade mark for office stationery, the name of a regular street market in London, and of an art gallery in Aberdeen; there may also be a solicitors' firm named "Fellowes", an unregistered trade mark for "Fellowes" kitchen utensils, and a registered one for garden seed and other equipment. And there may be yet more different entities equally entitled to the same mark in other countries around the world. Only one of these organisations will be able to register the name "Fellowes.com", and given the international nature of the Internet, that registration will be for world-wide use. The controversy is over who gets that domain name and why. The very delicate balance between territorial rights, classes of goods and services for which trade marks are registered, and requirements of confusion for infringement purposes, all of which provide a check on the monopoly power granted to owners of registered trade marks, is thus being upset.

Part of the dispute has arisen because of the way in which domain names are allocated. NSI, the body charged with overall responsibility for domain names in the USA, created an allocation policy under which domain names were registered on the basis that the first person to apply should be allocated the name (see *http://rs.internic.net/policy/internic/internic-domain4.txt* for the latest revision of this policy, and Oppendahl 1995, 1996a and b, for perceptive discussion). However, if a second party came along claiming to have superior right to the name because it had a registered trade mark which was the same as the domain name, the domain name holder might have to forfeit the domain name to the registered trade mark holder. A registered trade mark from any authority was sufficient for NSI. This meant that when a dispute arose, the holder of the domain name, but perhaps not a registered trade mark, did everything possible, and that at great speed, to obtain a registration of a trade mark and thus keep the domain name. An interesting test for the system was provided by Road Runner Computer Systems (RRCS), a company which offered Internet services. In December 1995, Warner Bros, owner of the registered trade mark "Road Runner", complained to NSI about the registration and use by RRCS of the domain name "roadrunner.com". NSI informed Roadrunner that the domain name would be placed on hold. Roadrunner then applied for, and got a trademark registration in Tunisia, which, unlike most other countries, will register a trade mark within a matter of days. However, NSI still refused to allow Roadrunner to keep the domain name. It was this policy of re-allocating the domain names to the registered trade mark owner that brought a number of disputes in the USA to a head. The policy completely ignored any claims that prior unregistered mark owners may have had, and also assumed that a domain name and a trade mark were synonymous.

Domain names - the disputes and the decided cases

Some companies which wanted to register a domain name in the ".com" top-level domain found that their preferred name had already been taken by someone else. The most obvious grounds for legal redress was to use trade mark law where there was a perceived similarity between a domain name and a registered trade mark.

The basis on which actions for infringement of trade marks by the use of domain names have been brought in the USA rest on two main grounds: confusion and dilution. The cases which rest on confusion, such as *Maritz Inc v Cybergold Inc* (1996 US Dist Lexis 14977, 29 August 1996), have looked at the underlying goods and services which have been in dispute and applied traditional principles of trade mark law and confusion. Maritz alleged trade mark infringement against CyberGold. Maritz had the unregistered "GoldMail" name and used it in conjunction with its GoldMail service on the Internet. CyberGold were developing a similar Internet service, using the domain name "cybergold.com". The court considered the matter of trade mark confusion, but found that in this case it was not proved.

Much more difficult have been the cases which have based themselves on trade mark dilution. The US Trade Mark Dilution Act 1995 has been used in a number of trade mark/domain name cases since its introduction in January 1996. In *Hasbro Inc. v Internet Entertainment Group Inc* (Case C96 130 WD), the court granted a preliminary injunction preventing Internet Entertainment Group from using the domain "candyland.com" for its website, which featured sexually explicit materials. Hasbro produces a game "Candy Land" for young children, and the court was persuaded that 94% of mothers were aware of this game. The court, perhaps influenced by the sexually explicit nature of the materials on the "candyland.com" website, found that the name "Candy Land" was being diluted through its use by others as a domain name on the Internet.

The Hasbro case concerned the use of a domain name which related to the underlying goods. Other cases on dilution have dealt with intentional hi-jacking of domain names that others use as trade marks in the course of business. An example is *Intermatic v Dennis Toeppen* (No 96 C 1982 ND 1 II). Dennis Toeppen registered the domain name "intermatic.com". The court found that the Intermatic mark was famous within the meaning of the Federal Trade Mark Dilution Act 1995; Mr Toeppens' use of that mark was commercial, as evidenced by his intention to resell or license the domain name; and the use of the name in connection with the Internet constituted "commerce" under the 1995 Act. By attempting to license or sell the mark, Toeppen "caused dilution of the distinctive quality of the mark by lessening Intermatic's capacity to identify its goods to potential customers and destroying the mark's advertising value".

This reasoning suggests that the courts in the USA would find dilution of a trade mark in all cases where there was an intention by the person who registered the name to sell it. A very similar approach is likely to be taken in the UK. In *Direct Line Group Ltd v Direct Line Estate Agency* (Chancery Division, 12 September 1996), a trade mark infringement action was brought against the directors of a number of companies with such names as YSL Limited and the Nike Clothing Company Limited. Direct Line Group Limited were objecting to the registration of the names Direct Line Estate Agency Limited and Direct Line Estates Limited. Laddie J said:

> [The directors] have a track record of taking or being associated with the taking of famous trade marks belonging to third parties, either for the purpose of carrying on business which siphons off the goodwill belonging to other traders, or for the purpose of offering those marks back to their rightful proprietors, no doubt at a profit. I think it only right to say that this court will view with extreme displeasure any attempt by traders to embark upon a scam designed to make illegitimate use of other companies' trade marks.

Even without full analysis of the question as to whether a domain name and trade mark are really synonymous, such a robust approach is to be welcomed in circumstances where one person intentionally pirates a domain name with the intention of trading on the goodwill of another or of holding them to ransom. However, there has been no analysis of the solution where there are two or more traders, both claiming the domain name, and both with equally valid claims to the registered trade mark, whether from within one jurisdiction, or from different countries around the world.

Trade Marks and Domain Names: the UK

There have been two cases on domain names that have reached court so far in the UK. The first was *Harrods Ltd v UK Network Services Ltd and Others* (High Court, Ch D December 9, 1996) (see Gardner 1997: 23). Michael Lawrie registered the address "harrods.com". Harrods, the well-known London department store, sued for trade mark infringement and passing off. Sadly, when the case called, the defendants did not turn up and so Harrods were given judgment by default. While the result was a victory for Harrods, the case has not furthered knowledge or understanding of trade mark and domain name law in the UK.

The second was *Pitman Training Limited and PTC Oxford Ltd v Nominet UK Ltd and Pearson Professional Ltd.* (High Court Ch D 22 May 1997) (for which see *http://www.open.gov.uk/1cd/scott.htm*). The dispute in this case was over the domain name "pitman.co.uk", which was claimed by Pearsons plc, who operate a publishing business, and Pitman Training Limited, who operate a training and correspondence course business. Both were equally entitled to use the name "Pitman" in the UK within their respective spheres of business. This case differs from the hitherto litigated trade mark and domain name cases, in that neither party had a registered trade mark. Rather the dispute was based on the common law tort of passing off, with Pitman Training Limited arguing that because they had used the domain name for a period of months, the general public would associate that name with their business, and should it revert to Pearsons plc, that would constitute passing off. The court disagreed that a case of passing off had been established on the rather thin evidence presented (two email messages had been sent to Pitmans during the months that the site had been in operation) and ordered that the domain name should be allocated to Pearsons plc on the basis that they had registered it first with Nominet.

So far, we have only seen the tip of the iceberg in relation to disputes over trade marks and domain names. A quick search of the Internet brings hundreds of addresses of websites containing information about disputes in this area, mainly from the USA, although there are indications that the numbers of disputes in the UK are on the increase, an example being *Prince plc v Prince Sportswear Group Inc.* (for which see *http://www.prince.com/prince*). Unfortunately, there has been little analysis by the courts to date as to whether trade mark law is applicable to the domain name dispute. Are trade marks and domain names synonymous? Or have commercial concerns latched on to this avenue as a suitable means to further their own competitive commercial aims? Are they now using trade mark law as yet another weapon in the armoury for shaping the Internet as a whole to suit their own ends?

Assuming that trade mark law is relevant, not all avenues have been explored in the search for the basis on which actions could be brought under trade mark legislation. For instance, in the UK, section 56 of the Trade Marks Act 1994 has provisions which suggest that famous names can be protected against trade mark dilution in the context of the Internet. If a person can show that his mark is "well known" in the UK then, regardless of whether he carries on business or has goodwill in the UK, he may stop a third party using a similar mark in relation to identical or similar goods, where that use is likely to cause confusion. What standard of proof this will require is not known, although Cornish (1996: 542) suggests that the methodical German approach, requiring 80% recognition, may set the standard. Objection can also be made under section 5(3) of the 1994 Act to the use of the mark in connection with dissimilar goods or services, such as Internet services, if it can be shown that the name has a reputation in the UK, and that the use of the name by a third party took unfair advantage of, or caused detriment to their own mark, a type of dilution.[5]

The implications are immense. Once a mark is well-known in one country, then that mark may not be used in any other country which is a signatory of the Paris Convention, whether or not the mark is well-known in *all* the signatory states. This is because a domain name is for world-wide use, and certainly any use in the country in which it was well-known would infringe. Taking the argument to its logical conclusion, ultimately only one trade mark may be used for one type of good or service in any one country in the world; the carefully structured territorial rights of the present regime become a *de facto* world-wide monopoly in the mark which no other trader may use, however dissimilar his goods or services.

In an attempt to try and bring order in this chaos, a regulatory body has been set up by a group of interested participants on the Internet, the International Ad Hoc Committee (IAHC). Membership includes the Internet Society (ISOC), the Internet Assigned Numbers authority (IANA), the Internet Architecture Board (IAB), the Federal Networking Council (FNC), the International Trademark Association (INTA) and the World Intellectual Property Organisation (WIPO). The IAHC has made a number of suggestions, including proposals to increase the number of generic top-level domains to seven, including ".firm" for businesses and ".store" for those offering to sell goods. The intention is that the most popular existing top-level domains, in particular the ".com" domain, will cease to attract so many disputes. A number of arguments suggest that that unlikely to work. Firstly, a number of businesses argue that they may lose associated goodwill if they are not able to use the ".com" domain, such is the current fixation on that example. Secondly, there are already over 230 top-level domains, but this has not alleviated the problem. Thirdly, there is no reason to suppose that some business will not simply register under all the top-level domains. It is still difficult to imagine that the owners of certain names would be happy in seeing their marks used by others. Harrods of London may now have "harrods.com", but that is unlikely to stop them from objecting to "harrods.firm" or "harrods.info" being registered by someone else. It will still be argued that confusion and dilution are present.

A further, interesting development is the proposal that has surfaced from the IAHC to the effect that the second domain name in the generic top-level domains will only be allocated to those parties who have "demonstrable intellectual property rights" in that name. The obvious question arises as to what is meant by "demonstrable intellectual property rights"? Does it mean a registered trade mark right, as favoured by NSI? Does it mean the applicant would need to have a right under passing off or its equivalent? It is hard to see how this proposal in its current form could serve to alleviate the potential disputes, as the cases to date have in any event been based on some form of intellectual property rights. It is the clash between these rights, coupled with the international nature of the disputes, that would appear irreconcilable.

Almost before the ink has dried on the paper, national regulators are arguing about whether this will solve the problems, creating a schism in the attempts to provide an international coherent solution. Thus Madeleine Albright, the American Secretary of State, has already said that the USA should not rush to accept the solution proposed because it may not be in the best interests of

American participants in this area to do so (for which see *http://secretary. state.gov/www/statement/*, and for comment *http://www.news.com/News/Item/ 0,4,10198,00.html*).

Conclusion

The development of new technologies has always posed exciting challenges for intellectual property law. Copyright, in particular, has managed to expand to provide protection for such media as films, television, sound recordings and computer software while at the same time maintaining a balance between the interests of the creators and users. The Internet is the latest development, drawing to itself applications of copyright and trade mark law and no doubt other, as yet unforeseen branches of this discipline. The Internet is challenging the justifications for intellectual property protection, and these are shifting. The concern is that the checks and balances between right-holders and users are being altered in a piecemeal manner without consideration of the effects on the overall structure of this branch of law.

A number of approaches, both short- and long-term, could be taken to ensure either that development of the Internet is not hampered either by over-regulation, or that it does not implode under the weight of litigation:

Firstly, as mentioned above, the Internet grew in a free and liberal manner, developed by users rather than by commercial interests. Given this basis of development, there are good arguments to dictate that the policy taken by the courts when faced with a dispute should be in favour of freedom rather than strict application of intellectual property laws drafted at a time when the Internet was, at most, in an embryonic state. This would permit, for example, creative development of the use of implied licences.

A slightly longer-term approach would be to develop one set of rules for commercial users of the Internet and another for non-commercial users. An embryonic form of this solution can be seen in the development of the transient reproduction right, and the suggestion mooted above that there should be infringement of this right only where the offending activity had an economic effect upon the commercial right-holder. The non-commercial user would be otherwise free to use the Internet in such manner as she sees fit. The main danger with this type of approach is that it is likely to increase transaction costs as questions surface about where the division of commercial and non-commercial lies.

A longer-term strategy still may be to develop a general law of unfair competition applicable to the Internet. A number of disputes discussed above, particularly the *Shetland Times* and the Ticketmaster/ Microsoft cases, would have been dealt with more happily under a general law of unfair competition had such an action been available, rather than by stretching the parameters of intellectual property law to meet rather dubious ends. The development of a discrete set of rules specifically aimed at the Internet has so far been resisted by many commentators. The initial question was whether existing intellectual property laws applied to Internet activities. Once it was accepted that they did, there was and is a reluctance to move on and say that something else should now be developed instead. However, given the current melee; the ad hoc responses of regulatory authorities; the stretching of existing intellectual property laws; and the battles for commercial supremacy, it is time to rethink this strategy. A new approach would have the advantage of being able to take an overview of the needs and interests of all those involved in the Internet: the right-holders, the users, those who provide the equipment, and the regulatory authorities, ultimately providing a framework for future sustained development of the Internet.

Notes

1 This argument was forcefully stressed in both *Cubby Inc v Compuserve Inc* 776 F Suppl 135 (1991) and *Stratton Oakmount Inc v Prodigy Services Company* 1995 NY Misc 23 Media Law Rep 1794, both concerning liability of service providers for dissemination of defamatory statements on the Internet.
2 The argument does not apply where infringing information is placed on the Internet–i.e. where it is placed there without the authorisation of the owner of the copyright, whether or not the owner of the copyright would have authorised the activity in the first place. In these circumstances different considerations apply, and the copyright owner should be free to sue those who place the information on the Internet in the first place. For an example in relation to unauthorised infringements of copyright see 'Rock band threatens to sue over Internet copyright', *Financial Times*, 8 May 1997.
3 Copyright Designs and Patents Act 1988 section 7 defines cable programme as 'any item included in a cable programme service'. A cable programme service is defined as 'a service which consists wholly or mainly in sending visual images, sounds or other information by means of a telecommunications system, otherwise than by wireless telegraphy, for reception (a) at two or more places (whether for simultaneous reception or at different times in response to requests by different users) or (b) for presentation to members of the public; and which is not, or so far as it is not, excepted by or under the following provisions of this section.
'The following are excepted from the definition of "cable programme service": a service or part of a service of which it is an essential feature that while visual images, sound or other information are being conveyed by the person providing the service there will or may be sent from each place or reception, by means of the same system or (as the case may be) the same part of it, information (other than signals sent for the operation or control of the service) for reception by the person providing the service or other persons receiving it.'
4 Fred Rosen, President and Chief Executive of Ticketmasters, said, 'You don't want them at your front door, and then find them in your bedroom' (*http://www.callaw.com/ticket.html*).

5   But note *Baywatch Production Co Ltd v The Home Video Channel* [1997] FSR 22 where the High Court considered the ambit of s 10(3) of the Trade Marks Act 1994 which is the mirror of s 5(3), but deals with infringement of marks with 'a reputation in the UK'. The court said that s 10(3) only applied where:
   1. A sign which is similar to the trade mark, so that there is a likelihood of confusion on the part of the public is used in relation to goods and services which are not similar to the mark; and
   2. the mark has a reputation in the UK; and
   3. the use of the sign, being without due cause, takes advantage of, or is detrimental to the distinctive character or the repute of the trade mark.

   It was the view of the court that the section introduced a requirement of likelihood of confusion on the part of the public. The case has been criticised, as there is no reference to confusion in the wording of the section.

Bibliography

Cornish, W. R., (1996). *Intellectual Property: Patents, Copyright, Trade Marks and Allied Rights*. 3rd edn. London: Sweet & Maxwell.
Gardner, N., (1997). The Harrods case: protecting your name on the Internet. *Computers and Law*, **8**, 23-26.
Goldberg, M., (1997). The new WIPO treaties: a report on the December 1996 Diplomatic Conference: the WIPO Copyright Treaty and the WIPO Performances and Phonograms Treaty. Unpublished paper presented at the Fifth Annual Conference on International Intellectual Property Law and Policy, Fordham University School of Law, New York, 3 and 4 April.
Oppendahl, C., (1995). Avoid the traps in the new rules for registering a domain name. *New York Law Journal*, 8 August (*http://www.patents.com/nylj3.sht*)
Oppendahl, C., (1996a). NSI domain name dispute policy puts owners at significant risk. *New York Law Journal*, 21 May (*http://www.patents.com/nylj6.sht*)
Oppendahl, C., (1996b). Fourth domain name policy leaves owners with few options. *New York Law Journal*, 3 September (*http://www.patents.com/nylj7.sht*)

THE QUARTERLY JOURNAL OF THE DAVID HUME INSTITUTE

HUME PAPERS ON PUBLIC POLICY

Access an authoritative overview of economic and legal aspects of public policy questions – subscribe to the **Hume Papers on Public Policy**. The quarterly journal of The David Hume Institute, the journal deals with topical issues of a national and international nature in a scholarly but accessible way. While the Institute has no political affiliations, it is particularly interested in encouraging analysis of the interaction between man-made institutional/legal framework of society and market forces – with special reference to economic well-being.

Make sure of your copies – fill in the form overleaf and return it to the address shown to receive the **Hume Papers on Public Policy** four times a year.

Selected articles

Sexual Equality

Money Laundering

Universities, Corporate Governance, Deregulation

In Search of New Constitutions

Scotland and the Union

Privacy and Property

Law on the Electronic Frontier

Managing Doctors

Copyright, Competition and Design

Deregulation and Privatization

Corporate Governance

Drug Trafficking and the Chemical Industry

Financing Devolution

Fraud on the European Budget

European Monetary Union

Deep Water: Fisheries Policy for the Future

HOW TO ORDER

HUME PAPERS ON PUBLIC POLICY

Make sure of your copies! Fill in this form and return it to the address below to receive the **Hume Papers on Public Policy** four times a year. Please tick the relevant boxes.

❏ Please enter my subscription to the **Hume Papers on Public Policy** Volume 5 1997, ISSN 1350-7516

Subscription rates

Institutional
❏ UK/EC £76.00
❏ N. America $140.00
❏ Rest of World £83.00

Individual
❏ UK/EC £38.00
❏ N. America $70.00
❏ Rest of World £42.50

Name _____
Address _____
_____
_____
_____ Postcode _____
Tel _____
Fax _____
E-mail _____

Method of Payment
❏ I enclose a cheque made payable to Edinburgh University Press
❏ Please debit my Visa/MasterCard

Card number _____
Expiry date _____

Signature _____

HP705/3

Return to:
Journals Marketing Edinburgh University Press,
22 George Square, Edinburgh EH8 9LF
Tel: (0044) 131 650 6207   Fax: (0044) 131 662 0553

EU Authorised Representative:
Easy Access System Europe Mustamäe tee 50, 10621 Tallinn, Estonia
gpsr.requests@easproject.com

Printed and bound by CPI Group (UK) Ltd, Croydon, CR0 4YY
22/03/2026
02076195-0002